Acknowledgements

I give thanks to the many people who have supported me with their enthusiasm and contributions when this book was little more than a set of sketchy thoughts:

To Liz and my daughters Jacqui and Jane, who in times long gone by tolerated my periodic absences from our family life in favour of my work in ABK's studio ('Daddy's in the Ovice').

To Marlene Rolfe who, having read my early manuscript, made a strong, clear proposal for the simplification of the voices in the text – a good moment.

This was followed by the architectural insight and wide-ranging excellence of Ian Latham's work as publisher and editor, progressing through each stage with fresh ideas, enthusiasm and a subtle consideration of my take on the subject. Thank you Ian, it's been a very rewarding experience.

To Christina Thornley who, seemingly undaunted by my awkward ways of expressing myself in difficult handwriting, put it all onto the computer in good spirit.

To members of my extended family: in Spain my sister Katy Ahrends, for gathering up her mother's photos of my father Steffen's Spanish work; in South Africa my cousin Ganga Thiel, who directed me to letters by and about my grandfather Bruno; and in Germany my cousins Christian Hallmann, Fritjof Sachs and his wife Katrin Sachs for helping access photos of Bruno's work.

My thanks to Jasper Donat who generously agreed to the publication of his father John Donat's photos of ABK's work; to the RIBA, where John's archive is held; and to Valerie Bennett and Byron Blakeley of the Architectural Association's slide library, where ABK's photo archive is held. Thanks also to Christine Cadin for the recent portrait photo, and George Kasabov for supplying a photo of one of your kilim rugs.

Finally, I want to express my overarching gratitude for the lifelong good fortune that I've experienced in working closely with my friends and partners, Richard Burton and Paul Koralek, in our determined effort to make good architecture.

Peter Ahrends

Peter Ahrends

A3
Threads and Connections

6	**Threads and Connections**
8	**A3: Three Generations**
14	**Unifying South Africa's Post-Apartheid Cities?**
18	**In South Africa as a Boy – 1937-51**
24	**London, a New Life and the Stuff of Architecture**
34	**ABK: Dialogue, Consultation and Collaboration**
46	Gathering Places
48	Clusters and Groupings
50	Entrances
52	Internal Routes
54	Two-Sidedness
58	Four-Square Buildings
62	Squared Cross Grids
64	Walls and Roofs
70	Rooflighting
74	A Poetic Dimension
78	**Bruno Ahrends: a Berlin Architect**
94	**Steffen Ahrends: Berlin, Moscow, Johannesburg and Andalucia**
108	**An Early Childhood in Berlin**
112	**A Grounded Afterword**
122	**Presence and Absence**

Threads and Connections

Until quite recently I hadn't even contemplated writing this book. It examines certain aspects of the life and work of three successive generations of twentieth century architects in my family. My grandfather, my father and I had left Nazi Berlin in the late 1930s, and each of us went on to live in different countries at different times. Having enjoyed a full life in London, working at Ahrends Burton & Koralek on projects that achieved some recognition over the years, a family-oriented dimension to my architectural life gradually began to make itself felt.

In the late 1960s, relatively early in our practice, I was working with Michael Hollings, a priest at the Roman Catholic Chaplaincy at the University of Oxford and our client for its new building. Realising that I was neither a religious believer nor well informed about the Liturgical Movement, Michael suggested that I should visit some of the new catholic churches that had been built in West Germany during the post-war period.

Around the same time our practice had been invited to attend a competitive interview for the design of the new National Theatre on London's South Bank. We had no working experience of theatre design, so in visiting Berlin it seemed sensible to also visit some of the city's new performance spaces. This would be my first trip back to the city of my birth since I'd left, aged three.

I felt deeply uncomfortable in Berlin, but I managed to avoid the critical question of why this was so. Walking through the city the presence of the infamous Wall certainly struck home, but only faintly did I appreciate that there may have been more to my discomfort.

I hired a VW to make a visit out of the city and, on my return, found myself caught in a long tailback on the autobahn, and saw that a police patrol was making its way along the lines of cars ahead, checking papers. Approaching me with their requests I searched in several pockets for passport, licence and car papers, not a model of confident efficiency. Our verbal exchange, my stumbling answers to the police officers' questions, did nothing to diffuse the growing tension. For no good reason I began to associate them with a stereotypical image of Nazi Party SS officers. Still here, are they? Crazy, prejudiced thoughts.

The police moved on to the driver of the Merc behind as I, 'not guilty', smouldered from the long-contained anger of my childhood eviction, now riding high with my sense of rebelliousness against authority.

I returned to London, well briefed on the subjects I'd set out to research. Knowing so little of my grandfather's work, however, I'd come away without looking out his buildings. For the moment, I felt that this was all that I could handle. I didn't understand then that, as a result of my extended family's difficulties in remaking their lives following their widespread emigrations, the folds of an emotionally-woven curtain of near-silence still separated me from my past. The curtain remained closed, almost.

Over the following years I made visits to various German cities in connection with other projects: a competition, the opening of an exhibition of ABK's work and a lecture. It seemed that I had cooled; no further autobahn scenes.

In the mid-1980s, Prince Charles attacked our competition-winning design for the National Gallery extension, and my name figured in the media for a while. This led to my unexpected receipt of several letters about my grandfather Bruno. One asked about his wartime stay in England (including his internment in Douglas on the Isle of Man), and another was from a student at Berlin's Technical University who was writing a dissertation on his work. Setting out the scope of her study she asked whether I might be able to help. Bit by bit Bruno's life began to acquire a more meaningful structure for me, from his work in Berlin during the Bauhaus period through to the design ideas drawn in his Douglas Camp sketchbooks. Studying his work further began to offer me a new relationship with this long-absent family, first with Bruno, and in due course with my father Steffen, who worked in Berlin and Moscow in the 1930s before emigrating to South Africa.

By the late-1980s fundamental political forces were shifting in eastern Europe, signalling the winds of change in the German Democratic Republic. After the Berlin Wall came down in 1989 I returned to see the city afresh, to visit Bruno's buildings, to do some work, to meet my hitherto unknown cousins and to make new friends.

Unbeknown to me, the embryo of this book came along too – seemingly to write itself. Well, that was the idea…

Peter Ahrends, London, June 2015

A3: Three Generations

I'm absorbed by an uncertainty. What's the underlying question? Is this just another story about a journey? Well, sort of, but that doesn't seem quite right. The journeys we make are usually structured events, travelling from place to place – London, Venice, Hong Kong or wherever – doing things, meeting people, seeing places, and we return with a sense of completion or achievement. This is a different sort of story. It reflects on the moments of connection in the migratory movements of three generations of architects.

It begins in Berlin, where my grandfather Bruno established his practice following the first world war. After the Nazis closed his office in 1937, he uprooted first to Italy before fleeing to England in 1939 only to be interned on the Isle of Man. Shortly before his death in 1948 he emigrated to Capetown. My father Steffen had been born in Berlin in 1907, and following an interlude in Moscow moved to Johannesburg, and then towards the close of his working life to Andalucia. I too was born in Berlin, and brought up in Johannesburg before relocating alone to London in my late teens. Intriguingly, the work of these three generations of architects came to be linked as much with twentieth century political ideologies as their cultural contexts.

Unlike writing or painting, architecture is seldom done alone, although ideas swirl around in the mind of the individual, searching, sketching, testing and nurturing unresolved bits in an amalgam of the imagination. This almost tangible sense of 'doing' within a dynamic of group interaction characterises the essence of design activity. Imaginations stir and move as the development of iterative stages of early design ideas encourage and sustain a process of collaboration.

Above
The childrens' street game of hopscotch dates back to Roman times, since when variations have developed throughout the world, from India to Peru.

Left
Berlin's Brandenburg Gate and Unter den Linden before the Wall was built, and the Wall's final days in 1989. From 1961-89 the Berlin Wall divided the east and west sectors of the former German capital. Viewed from the east as an 'Anti-Fascist Protection Rampart' and from the west as the 'Wall of Shame', it symbolised the 'Iron Curtain' of the Cold War.

So architecture is in my blood, not just through the disturbed life patterns of this Berlin family, but equally in my working life with my partners in Ahrends Burton Koralek over a period of fifty years. But 'in my blood' evokes other powerful meanings, not least in the pulsating rhythms of movement in city life. Accelerating surges of unprecedented urban growth across the globe reinforce our recognition of the meanings of the city in our lives; energies flowing in the veins and arteries of that most fundamental and binding of human inventions where, en masse, we make places. Seemingly beyond our control, the scale and intensity of new layers of city growth describe who we are in relation to the fabrics and character of our urban past. Earlier temples, palaces, power stations, porticos and triumphal arches spoke of an authority whereby dressed stonework, weight and mass described ordered ways of making it clear who was who. And in the suburbs, where in earlier times children drew lines of chalk, the rhythms of bouncy hopscotch movements followed traditional game-playing patterns. Walking by, did we pause to watch these dance lessons in architecture on our pavements?

Strolling through our city streets there's little evidence of our developing understanding of the science of multiverses, dark energy and matter, nor the marvel of that show-stopping expansion of the universe. Why raise this when it's the art, grit and grain of imaginations that make architecture's new urban places? Is there more to find? Yes, for with fresh sight and analysis the social dimensions of urban work reveal underlying conceptual strands.

Images of possible new fragments in our cities and their significance in the flow and make-up of ceaseless urban change bring to mind an idea that I instigated when teaching at the Bartlett School of Architecture (at University College London) in the late 1980s. The school's entire student body would work for a period of several years on a series of projects hinged conceptually around the idea of 'patchwork'. The projects would be set in one district of London in the first year, then in another the following year (a historic part of Southwark, then a linear stretch between King's Cross and Paddington stations, for example). In due course the programme would constitute a patchwork of urbanism, interpreted and imagined across the whole school from the early years through to the final year diploma thesis. The intention was not to make a city plan nor a proscribed structure for urban growth, but rather a progressively responsive set of design snapshots, illustrating developing skills of complexity within a collective student diary of ideas. The interrogative process of making buildings from their essential elements – foundations, columns, beams, floors, walls and roof – could initially serve as a kind of lexicon of assembly, and ultimately look to the development of urban areas by encouraging a gradual appreciation of the formal and spatial meanings of new parts in relation to an existing whole.

I first came to appreciate something of these kinds of relationships in my late teens when, working on building sites as an apprentice carpenter and plumber, I experienced the assembly of parts in relation to the materiality of the whole. This found resonance in later years, studying the collective weavings of Turkish kilim rugs in which the geometric dynamic of patterns are brought to completion, rug by rug, by small formal and colour variations at the hands of each weaver. And, closer to our western cultural traditions, the collective making of patchwork quilts, where a diversity of patterned bits, made with skill and imagination, form delightful and unpredictable combinations.

Is there not some parallel in the patchwork of human relations that forms the subject of this book? Like many other families, mine was scattered and set apart by the threat of Nazism. Pushed, pulled and stretched across place and time, my interest lies now in the recovery of possible connections, not so much in an attempt to suggest a whole, but rather to assemble a loose-fit but linked storyline.

Occasionally, accidental connections seem to happen, like pointers to snippets of an unknown family history. As a third year student at the Architectural Association, I found myself walking across a stretch of open land in Kidbrooke, south-east London, in the company of Arthur Korn, my tutor for a housing design project. Korn, we soon learned, was without equal in his infectious and well-informed enthusiasm for the Modern Movement. He turned to ask my name. 'Ahrends… Ahrends…', he mused in a distinctive German accent of the kind familiar to me since childhood. Learning that I had been born in Berlin and taken to South Africa by my emigrating parents in 1937, he asked whether I was related to Bruno. Yes, but I hadn't seen my grandfather since the age of three. Spontaneously and engagingly he spoke of Bruno's housing projects in Berlin. They'd known one another through Der Ring, the progressive group established in Berlin in 1926 by architects including Hugo Häring, Walter Gropius and Mies van der Rohe, and dissolved under pressure from the Nazi regime in 1933. From today's perspective it's difficult to get a sense of what the inter-war cultural buzz of Berlin must have been like. There, Korn had made his mark as an architect, before emigrating to the UK and teaching at the AA in the post-war years. There

Right
Illustration from a Soviet-era childrens' booklet, purchased in Moscow by his parents for their soon-to-be-born son Peter.

Left
Kilim rugs (from the Persial 'gelim', meaning 'to spread roughly'), are woven with wool and cotton to produce a flat surface without piles. Made from the Balkans to Pakistan, they usually feature striking geometric designs in bold colours (ph: George Kasabov).

Below
Arthur Korn (1891-1978) was a German Jewish architect and urban planner. He emigrated to London in 1938, where he joined the MARS Group (Modern Architecture Research), and taught at the Oxford School of Architecture and, from 1945, the Architectural Association.

Above
Kurt Schwitters' portrait of Klaus Hinrichsen, a fellow detainee at the Hutchinson Camp.

he fired this student's developing aspirations with the strength of his convictions for the Modern Movement. Deeply felt and powerfully expressed, his spirit stays fertile in my mind.

More than thirty years later, I made another chance connection with Berlin, following Prince Charles' criticisms of ABK's competition-winning proposal for an extension to London's National Gallery. Amidst all the media attention I received a letter from Klaus Hinrichsen, an art historian who was working with Zuleika Dobson on the Art in Exile exhibition to be held at the Camden Arts Centre in London in 1986. Was I, he asked, Bruno Ahrends' son? Not his son, I replied, but his grandson. And did I have a portrait of Bruno or any material relating to his internment on the Isle of Man? Hinrichsen had been among the youngest at the Hutchinson Camp in Douglas where a remarkable gathering of emigres who, having fled Nazi Germany in the late 1930s, came to be interned by the British government in this remote spot. Culturally, it was a far cry from Berlin.

So, in the emotional turmoil that followed the cancellation of our National Gallery project, I faced an unexpected and unwanted recognition. The distant memory of my family's involvement with the Modern Movement in Berlin began to take on a more personal meaning. What had followed under Nazism, with Albert Speer's visions of the city along with ceremonial expressions of political power, the sweeping grandeur and assertion of the historic symbolisms of a bygone classical language was, I came to feel, no longer so disconnected from this three-year-old's loss of home.

Arthur Korn and Klaus Hinrichsen had known Bruno better than me, but meeting them helped me to reconnect with my past. These chance meetings, more than three decades apart, came to have more significance as I began to recognise the depth of my denial about my lack of family connections with this 'lost' homeland. During my childhood in South Africa these matters were left undiscussed, so even as a young adult I had no notion of this elephant occupying several rooms of my strangely fractured and globally extended family house.

Following our flight from Nazi Germany to South Africa, my parents seemed unable to recognise that a young child might need help in understanding the reasons for such a drastic change of circumstances. Was it too difficult? Were they unable to share their sense of loss in their struggle to make a new life?

During the post-war years in Johannesburg I was aware of my family's connection with a loose-knit community of German émigrés. Many were secular Jews who had foreseen what was to come and managed to leave, but also among them (unbeknown to me at the time) were non-Jewish families who had left for political reasons.

There may be nothing unusual or surprising about such social regroupings. This was a remote colony, a society deeply fractured by colonial racism long before apartheid policies came into effect in the late-1940s. For the ruling white minority this was a land of plenty, and not one that would have tolerated the politics of the left. For the immigrant Germans there was nothing like the culture they'd enjoyed in Berlin in the late-1920s and early-1930s, and this void may have had some unconscious effect on this young child.

While the émigrés had escaped Germany with their lives, it was not the whole of their lives. I can still recognise my childhood feelings about these architects, artists, craftspeople, intellectuals and historians. Their loosely shared culture was sufficiently different from the 'indigenous' colonial norm as to register and impress me, not least in relation to my muted sense of who I was and where I belonged.

How does this 'absence of belonging' figure in who I became, and in how I relate to those connections I later came to value? My immediate interest, however, lies less in who I am but rather in the connections between these loose-coupled sets of people, and especially in how their work developed during troubled times in different places.

Above
Johannesburg street scene in the 1930s.

Left
Model of Albert Speer's proposed north-south axis in Berlin – the Prachtstrasse or Street of Magnificence – with the domed Volkshalle at its north end and triumphal arch to the south. The outbreak of war in 1939 led to the abandonment of the plan.

Unifying South Africa's Post-Apartheid Cities?

Returning to South Africa for a short visit in 1993, I felt strong emotion as the queue moved slowly through passport control at Johannesburg airport. After the long night in a cramped aircraft seat from London, I was moved by the early morning sun rising over this land that with hindsight had come to mean so much to me.

I had left South Africa for London in July 1951, exchanging the politics of apartheid for an architectural education and feeling that this would mean the start of a new life on the British edge of Europe. Yet standing in the queue more than 40 years later, I feel moved. Then, apartheid held sway. Now, I get a first sense of the lifted spirits among the black faces. It had been three years since Nelson Mandela's release from Robben Island prison, and a year before he would become president. With the political system in transition, I was here to attend the African National Congress' International Solidarity Conference – and to experience the lift of this potent moment of global significance.

Little wonder that I was filled with emotion. Having been effectively evicted from Berlin by the Nazis 56 years earlier, I witness early signs of a great democratising change. Soon we'd see the downfall of the racist demons and the birth of a new democracy. Just four years earlier, the collective rise of the people in the German Democratic Republic had brought down the Berlin Wall. Here, the wall was the ideology of racist division, and now that too would be torn down.

I was attending the conference as chair of the campaigning group UK Architects Against Apartheid, (UKAAA), but what could I say about the role of architecture in this emerging new world? Modern architecture has often made powerful

Left
The Architects Against Apartheid (AAA) ran a long campaign to persuade the Royal Institute of British Architects (RIBA) to sever its links with all-white architectural institutions in South Africa. This led to RIBA's withdrawal of its recognition from the segregated architectural courses at South African universities. From the late 1980s, the group worked with colleagues in South Africa to consider projects for a post-apartheid era.

connections with the politics of democracy, not least in the state-funded health, housing and education building programmes of post-war Britain. Setting aside the classical language of temples and porticos that was employed to express elitism, the architects of the Modern Movement drew upon the aspirations of democracy in the search for new interpretations and meanings.

I'm an advocate of the Modern Movement of course, but at the same time keen to interrogate the influences of underlying political forces. Employing architecture as a means to express power is a well-trodden path – are the high-rise urban towers built by global banking businesses really that far removed from the Renaissance palaces built by the Medicis?

Each morning we conference delegates – a large and varied group from all around the world – were taken by coach from our downtown Johannesburg hotel to an out-of-town venue. This repetitive experience triggered a childhood memory of Africans being transported in dangerously overcrowded buses from the outlying townships to provide low-cost labour for the white-controlled cities. Even to relatively uncritical teenage eyes, the political significance of the oppression of the black majority by the white minority, each inhabiting sharply differentiated settlements, was pervasively evident.

During the conference I became increasingly aware of the need to think progressively and iteratively about the urban legacy of the Nationalist government's apartheid policy. The regime had built segregated African townships beyond the fringes of white-occupied towns and cities throughout the country. These were never too far distant, however, to ensure that control of the black labour force in contained, underprivileged and marginalised settlements was maintained. The political clarity of this awesome urban superstructure was being laid out and re-presented to me, a dichotomy whose distorted and ambiguous urban patterns crowded in on the mind. If nothing else, there was a need to investigate radically alternative types of city structures, and back in the hotel that evening I started to make a few notes and sketches.

The following morning, as we jogged along in the bus to the conference venue, I raised this emerging set of ideas with the veteran anti-apartheid campaigner and former prisoner Denis Goldberg who was sitting beside me. How can I begin the enormous task of assessing the post-apartheid cities, I asked him. 'Go to it', he said, 'just do it'.

Ridiculous, far too ambitious, and unachievable. How could I possibly unpick the history and structure of the townships? Realising however that I needn't tackle it in this way, it became clear that my first task was to think about the issues. In some respects the extraordinary scale and predominance of the problem was helpful rather than daunting, for here was a clear model of racial separation and urban division that went against every fibre of my civic being as well as my aspirations as an architect.

Returning to London, I shared the ideas with my colleagues at the UKAAA, but there was little enthusiasm. Rightly perhaps it was thought that we had more immediate, high-priority anti-apartheid projects. And, given the increasingly evident signs of a political interregnum (the new ANC government wasn't formed until 1994), the time didn't seem right for such a fundamental intervention.

The idea lost some of the energy of immediacy and was put on hold until the new government, led by Nelson Mandela, was fully instated and, in due course, I was able to speak with Joe Slovo, the new Minister for Housing. I had met Joe occasionally at relaxed dinners with friends during his exile in London. This time we had a delightful conversation about the wonder and significance of the ANC's achievement, punctuated by congratulations and expressions of joy. We hadn't been in touch for some time, and although I'd known something about Joe's role in the earlier period of the ANC struggle my ideas about the structure of cities were far beyond the usual after-dinner conversation. I outlined my initial thoughts, suggesting that I'd like to visit him in Pretoria to discuss them further. Joe paused. The initial focus, he said, had to be on the planning and delivery of a widespread housing provision, sewerage and other essential utilities. But, he added, the ideas sound interesting – let's plan to meet, perhaps in a year's time? Yes, I said, respecting his view of the country's more pressing housing need – yes, let's meet then.

Sadly Joe died the following year, tragically early in a political career and with his ambitions for his country far from realised. I like to think that Joe would have responded positively, if only because the issues were of such fundamental significance to the future of the nation's social well-being. With the benefit of hindsight, I now realise that I could have suggested that these ideas need not have disturbed the urgent focus on housing and infrastructure. On the contrary, their development could have provided a parallel course of design action while also offering a fundamentally different set of views that might have helped promote radical policies for settlements in the liberated post-apartheid state.

There's one more point of relevance to the project's slow progress. In the late-1980s, while I was professor at the Bartlett school of architecture at University College London (UCL), I chaired a core group of architects that set the policy directions of the UKAAA. Working with Mike Terry and Glen Robinson of the Anti-Apartheid Movement, I was invited to meet ANC activist Mendi Msimang to discuss how our group's work could best be coordinated so as to reinforce the ANC's political initiatives in the UK. In 1994 Mendi was appointed as South Africa's High Commissioner in London, based in South Africa House, overlooking Trafalgar Square and for long the seat of the 'enemy'. So it was that during Mendi's period of office that we met again, this time to discuss my ideas within a formal political framework over fine cups of tea. No longer, we thought, would this be a project destined to remain on paper. But we soon found that the process of diplomacy follows its own pace. Some years later, when Thabo Mbeki was president, we came close to meeting his deputy, but frustratingly this never happened. Not long afterwards, in 2008, Mbeki resigned, and although Glen and I have since attended several further meetings with key people in South Africa, as yet no serious move has been made.

Given the limits of a professional lifespan, what's the likely prognosis? Should we measure success by the implementation of ideas? Of course ideas are, in essence, simple to describe, but making them a reality would require fresh research, widespread consultation and determined political commitment.

The spatial separation of townships from the towns and cities was an explicit manifestation of the Nationalist's racist policy of apartheid. Imagine, if you can, the process of planning a place in which people are to be subjected to regimented mechanisms of brutal control. The implicit instruction must have been 'whatever you do, don't think that these planned townships are for normal human beings, communities and families. Don't think like that! They're not like you and me'.

Top
Joe Slovo (1926-95) was a long-time leader of the South African Communist Party (SACP), a leading member of the African National Congress (ANC), and a commander of the ANC's military wing. He lived in exile between 1963 and 1990, organising opposition to the Apartheid regime, including a period in London from 1966-78.

Above
Social campaigner Denis Goldberg (born 1933) was imprisoned for 22 years following the Rivonia Trial. After his release in 1985 he lived in London, working for the ANC. He returned to South Africa in 2002.

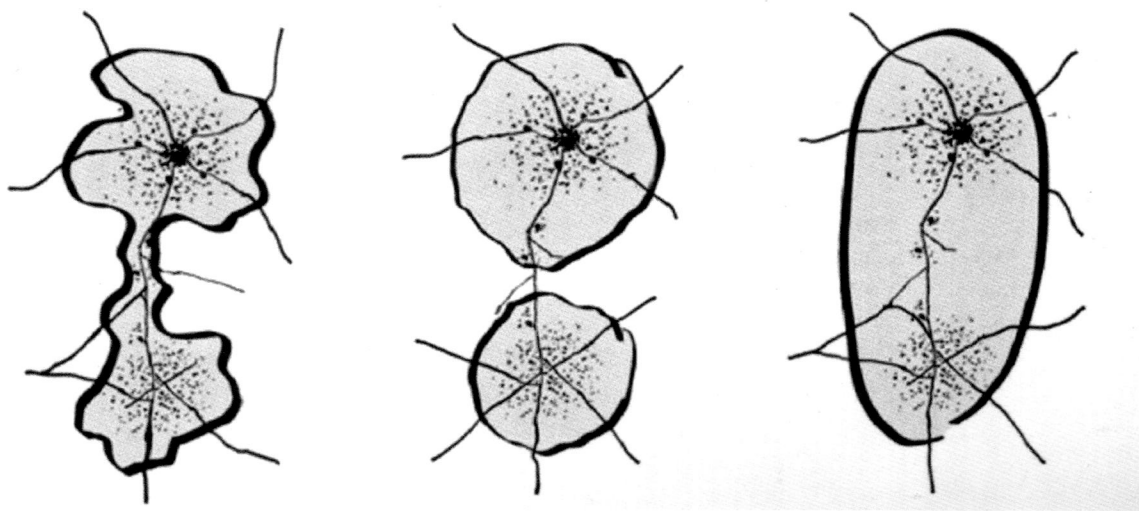

Above right
Peter Ahrends' initial sketch ideas for a post-apartheid study of planning options, intended to address the spatial separation of townships from their adjacent cities.

So what, we ask, is the government's policy for this bi-polar urban legacy? Things are changing, but the spatial separation remains and the townships still serve as powerful evocations of a grim past. What can be done to make a better urban world? The magnitude of the problem and the complexity of the urban conditions lead me to suggest that we shouldn't leave things to market forces. Only after research, consultation and the testing of ideas can we formulate imaginative proposals to support enlightened government policies to unify the townships and cities.

Whether there's a political context capable of embracing this breadth of vision, however, is debatable. Political power games and vested interests set the agendas and social needs are prioritised within such frameworks. Our ideas will retain their significance but we'll lose the game if no one in authority takes a serious interest. My instinct and commitment is to hang in there, to seek new ways of promoting positive action, and stimulate interest by discussion. A good start might be for the president to lend support to our 'Unifying Post-Apartheid Cities' study. We plan to set up a distinguished working group with universities and key agencies on the ground, and study the primary elements of the as-found situation, city by city. Consult, analyse, consider, draw up and describe clear options. Then, after feedback, evaluate and recommend. Guided by our aspiration and commitment, the project is achievable within a year. I like to think that Joe Slovo would have agreed with Denis Goldberg, challenging me to 'go to it'.

In South Africa as a Boy – 1937-51

We lived in a large house designed by my father on a remote hillside just beyond Northcliff, then an outer suburb of Johannesburg, at the edge of an open landscape of mountains and valleys. Returning home from primary school each day, I was free to roam in the heat of the rock-strewn terrain. This, for me, was Africa. A far cry from the Berlin apartment that had been my first home. Nor was it like the flat we shared temporarily with another émigré family in Johannesburg's downtown business area, a place I remember mostly for the rows of strangely motionless out-of-hours trolley buses close-parked outside.

Early each weekday amidst the bustle of the morning rush hour, my mother would settle me on a bus at the terminus, requesting the conductor and fellow passengers to put me off at the stop by my nursery school. A very young traveller introduced to the strange pattern of a daily journey, wondering why my mother seemed to abandon me each morning. Was she off to work? It wasn't clear to me then, and the question still hangs with me today.

I've skipped over the major part of our journey from Germany to South Africa. Curiously, I have no sure memories of the moment we left our home and extended family in Berlin. Nor even of my father's departure to Johannesburg several months earlier in search of work and a place to live.

So it was that I left Berlin with my mother to travel to Southampton where, I was later reminded, we met my beloved aunt Marianne who had come to see us off on a liner sailing to Capetown. My father's sister was a doctorate lawyer who, having been denied continuity of professional status by the Nazis, had come to live and work in London. I have a distinctive memory of the prow of the big ship lying still in Southampton's dockside scene. What kind of place can this be, I wondered?

Crossing the equator during the voyage, we children were organised to process down the central aisle of the ship's dining hall at the close of the grown-ups' evening meal, each carrying lanterns. I recall feeling uneasy about the formality of the ceremony; it was odd just being there without the slightest understanding of its meaning. No rehearsal, join the line, get on and do it. For a German lad with no English there must have been a language problem, but I have no recollection of any difficulty. Perhaps I'd been reassured by my mother telling me that the procession was to celebrate my fourth birthday which, coincidentally, was that day.

It's interesting to reflect on how the form and gravitas of such occasions carry meaning. And why does the powerful presence of an ocean liner impress a three-year-old who nonetheless lacks any understanding of its function?

At the end of each school day I walked home in the heat of the afternoon sun, trudging uphill through tall, dry grass, along the hard-baked veld path formed by the herd of pungent goats that I would encounter, grouped with their tinkling bells just below the plateau escarpment that was home. I would pause to study the insects. Beetles that tapped their dark brown abdomens on the hard path to attract a mate, and others that lurked in smooth inverted cones of sand to trap hapless ants.

This daily free-ranging wildlife adventure was my antidote to the regime of school. Being alone yet contained between the powerful expanse of land mass and the overriding breadth and blueness of an African sky there was, I now see, a developing sense of identity and of belonging. Not a city, just a community of creepy-crawlies, tiny local inhabitants

Above
In the 1930s, Southampton was described as the 'Gateway to the World'. The port handled half of the UK's ocean-going passenger traffic and millions of tons of cargo.

Above right
Watercolour sketch of the thatched bungalow, designed by Steffen Ahrends for his family in the suburbs of Johannesburg (1940).

Right
Plein Square, Johannesburg, in the 1950s.

Above
Mine dumps have been a feature of Johannesburg's suburban landscape since the 1886 gold rush. Today almost two million people live near the six billion tons of spoil, much of it toxic.

busy doing their thing along the winding route.

One day a vivid encounter occurred among these rocky outcrops. A large, honey-coloured boulder that I would enjoy clambering over had a distinctive fracture, an irregular crack dividing its mass into two. Drawn into the darkness of this jagged fault-line, I laid my cheek on the stone's sun-warmed surface, and froze as the steely, steady gaze of a pair of snake's eyes locked on me. We two were arrested, held by the fear and tension of surprise, and in that frozen moment I was unable to move. Living among these hills I knew enough about the danger of deadly snakes and eventually managed to pull myself away, leaving well alone. No thoughts of returning for another viewing; nor, later, of discussing the event with my parents. Alone, the only child copes.

Symbolically, this was an ordinary event loaded with content: the easy, recreational clambering opportunity that the boulder had offered, the unknown origin and meaning of the crack that formed a natural division in a great solid mass, the mysteriousness of its interior darkness and the unexpected danger of the serpent within – an adventure. Is it too fanciful to think that the evident but unexplained power of the boulder's fracture has had an influence on some of the underlying figures of my work: ambiguity, opposition, contradiction? I doubt my partners would agree, so for the moment I'll add an event of a different kind, from the end of my first year at the Architectural Association.

Our final project was to design a single-storey family house on an open plot of land, the converse of a tight urban condition where constraining contextual factors can offer a starting point. At the presentation, I explained my idea for a house of rectangular plan in which a prominent cross-wall divided the whole space into two parts, separating the living areas from bedrooms, and rising up well above the flat roof – a distinctive vertical plane to be made of stone.

I was encouraged by the positive comments of my tutor Leonard Manasseh during the crit, which he concluded with the remark that my formal proposition left open an 'unresolved duality'. The discussion ended but the observation, clearly prescient, lived on in a recurring preoccupation with dualities, the division of a whole and the potency of two significant parts, polarised yet synchronised. A year or two later, Charles Eames spoke at the AA about another duality: the binary number system that was the foundation of modern computing. I didn't understand the underlying maths but was excited by the implications.

When I was aged 11 and about to move on to secondary school, my parents divorced. The family home was abandoned and I became a boarder at a distinguished public school, a colonial version of the English model, situated in the Eastern Cape coastal city of East London. My new-found world, with its ambiguous expression of well-tended suburbia and the not-quite wildness of what lay beyond, was disturbed, removed.

I later learned that the wealthy acquaintance who had funded our family's journey to South Africa had advised my parents (who were agnostic if not atheist) to have me baptised: 'might be better', he'd said, 'you never know what you'll find'.

I was baptised in a Catholic church, and can remember the holy water trickling uncomfortably over my three-year old forehead. I had perceived no advantage from this during my first eight years in South Africa, but now my smart parents could truthfully claim in my boarding school application that I was a Catholic. In a school that was very white and Anglican, boys were expected to attend church service on Sunday mornings, and I was told that I was to be on my honour to instead attend the Catholic mass. Neglecting this godly guidance, I soon carried out my alternative Sunday plan to make the 800-mile train journey home to Johannesburg. I'd failed on the previous Sunday (with subsequent recriminations by a stern master), having arrived at the station just as the train steamed out. On my second attempt, with a fellow escapee – also a boarder who, I later learned, was Jewish and so also excused from Anglican worship – we made it just on time. With neither tickets nor money we moved at intervals, toilet by toilet, along the length of the train. To no avail, as later in the journey we were apprehended by a smart ticket collector.

The episode may say something about initiative and chutzpah, deviously good planning, an irreligious boy's view of formalised church attendance, perhaps a kind of controlled desperation, or just plain unhappiness. But it was the closing passage of this weekend adventure that had the most enduring significance for me.

On arrival at Johannesburg station we were led along the platform to the railway police office. Firmly though not unkindly we were grilled, and my concocted story about the sudden death of a grandmother unravelled. Parents were duly summoned by telephone and soon arrived to deal with everything, as parents do. But while we were waiting, through open doors, I saw another young boy being shunted into an adjacent office. Black and, I assumed, also caught without a ticket, he was being abused by another policeman, not violently but with physical and verbal aggression, a treatment from which my privileged white skin saved me.

My escape from boarding school, the long train

journey home, and the subsequent predicament with the railway police seemed as nothing compared with this double standard, the evident injustice of this racism, a word with which I was not yet familiar. This was 1944, several years before the Nationalist government came to power and enacted its inhuman policy of apartheid. I never knew the outcome of the young black boy's detention, but the power of the moment lived on in the mind. Nor did I ever meet my escape accomplice again. And while I knew that in some fundamental way my values had been shaken and shifted, I didn't know then what to do with this new understanding.

I was expelled by the school not, they made clear in a letter to my parents, because of my first near-miss escape 'offence' but because, in spite of the severe pep talk, this young boy did it again. Flouting authority, successfully.

It's possible that the experience of leaving Berlin with my parents during the rise of Nazi anti-semitism had given rise to the sense of injustice I felt at Johannesburg station. But at that young age I was unable to rationalise such injustice within a political framework – merely witnessing the bullying brutality seemed all I could handle at the age of 11.

A year or so later, after the end of the Second World War, my mother took me to see a black and white film that compiled newsreel of the Nazi concentration camps. Sitting there, rigid with fear at the horror of the images, I had no choice but to confront the brutal aspects of the politics of racism. But still this 12-year-old made no effective connections. And, of interest to me in later years, was the realisation that my parents, having fled Nazism and lived in Moscow in the early-1930s, then under the Stalin regime, never discussed their political views with me, nor did they share their feelings about these events. Too painful? And difficult, perhaps, when as German refugees in South Africa during the war years, they were experiencing their loss and departure from afar?

In another formative incident that framed my growing sense of the world, I was out in the local woods after school with a friend who was keen to show off his skill at shooting birds with a new pellet gun. When he didn't succeed, he urged me to have a go. I had never held a gun in my life, not even a toy. Looking up into the branches he spotted a bird, gave me instructions and I fired. The bird dropped to the ground. Where he was congratulatory, I was overwhelmed by a feeling of guilt and loss. The death of this small, still-warm, feathered creature, entitled to life, was all my doing.

Later I come to wonder about relationships between events, past and present. As Brooke Bayoude, a 10-year-old girl in novelist Ali Smith's book There But For The, says: 'And what I also want to know is, if something is in the past… can it still in any way be happening now?'. Late in life, recalling my early teenage feelings, I'm left with a recurring sense that, somehow, I then 'needed' to be elsewhere, to move beyond the limits of the emerging life pattern that was, unspoken, on offer.

The idea of leaving nudged its way into my consciousness. The alternative – to stay put and actively oppose the racist politic – hadn't occurred to me then, nor might it ever have done so from within that status quo. Instead I felt an undirected sense that I should move to Europe.

There was no way I could have seen myself returning to Berlin, so although the United Kingdom was evidently not part of Europe in 1951, I travelled to London. The Architectural Association had been recommended, my parents were

supportive, and with my experience of personal journeys I felt this was do-able. So it was – I travelled cheaply by boat up the east coast of Africa, calling at ports on the way before docking at the mind-blowing destination of Venice as the sun was setting one evening in early August. For five days I wandered and wondered, absorbing this city not yet overcome by tourism, a lone lad overwhelmed by the watery hugger-mugger of people and palaces.

My knowledge of the Renaissance was slight, but later, staying several weeks in Florence with friends, I found myself, untutored, favouring earlier periods of architecture and art – less loaded perhaps for this young mind. Was I drawn to modern architecture? Yes, but the real interest was yet to come, as was, during a later visit to Berlin, my discovery of grandfather Bruno's white architecture of the 1930s.

Left
Arriving at Venice on a hot August evening at sunset, Peter Ahrends was 'struck, in the days that followed, by the intensity of being alone in my experience of the city's water-based urban culture'.

London, a New Life and the Stuff of Architecture

At the end of August 1951 I travelled by train from Florence to London to enrol at the Architectural Association in Bedford Square. My head was loaded with kaleidoscopic memories of Venice and Florence – the criss-crossing of city fabrics, peopled places, the heat of stone enclosures, water and movement, blue-sky intensities of light and shade, the lingering incense of market tomatoes, and those cypresses punctuating the stepped rise to Fiesole. All seemed like another world on the grey, late afternoon as the winding suburban train trailed London's terraced slate roofs and brick chimneys before me. Although we must have crossed the Thames as we approached Victoria Station, I'm surprised that London's flowing lifeline didn't figure strongly in my first impressions.

Drab after my recent experiences? Intimidating for a young loner? Bewildered, certainly, by the complexity of this unfamiliar city, I couldn't yet comprehend my small significance within the magnitude of this agglomeration. Nor was I concerned with whether I'd find a comfortable kind of fit. Arriving alone and with my initial impressions of London's post-war austerity, I was youthfully uncertain yet seemingly unafraid.

Among my first experiences was a visit to the Festival of Britain, the great architectural showcase of the last years of Clement Attlee's remarkable post-war Labour government that had done so much to effect fundamental social change. Here I found a fresh and powerful sense of modernity, energy and optimism which, I was later to find, was where my 'sharp contrast' was to lie.

In my early years in the UK, working within the academic and student cultures that prevailed at the Architectural Association, the social dimension

Above, left
The Festival of Britain, held on London's South Bank in 1951, provided a showcase for a young generation of architects. Masterminded by Hugh Casson, the exhibition featured the temporary Dome of Discovery (by Ralph Tubbs) and the Skylon (by Powell & Moya with Felix Samuely).

Left
The principal focus of the 1951 Festival of Britain – the South Bank Exhibition – attracted more than eight million visitors, over half from outside London. The Festival was strongly associated with the Labour Party, which had won the 1945 general election, and it was opposed by the Conservative Party. Winston Churchill described the Festival as 'three-dimensional Socialist propaganda', and one of his first acts on becoming prime minister in October 1951 was to order the clearance of much of the South Bank site.

became a significant factor (as A, B and K progressively came together as a student group), and it came to form a key aspect of our work over the following five decades.

Obvious, you might think. For, in designing a school would we not be bound to consider, say, how the groupings of the classrooms and their character would express the relationships of individuals and groups to one another and, importantly, the ways in which these parts would relate to the complex as a whole? And how that whole is based upon and speaks about an interpretation of the aspirations set out in an educational policy?

In the period following my arrival in London I was hoping to explore a new ambition in the city in which I'd come to study architecture. Later, I hoped to engage with the stuff of making contributions to urban grains, modern punctuations which were sometimes, with good reason, radical. At other times, less assertive interventions might be needed, helping to establish places in which old and new buildings would become responsive neighbours.

Arriving at the Architectural Association – far removed from family and friends and the dry heat of the African land – was certainly a 'shock of the new' for this colonial lad. Perhaps above all, there was a barely recognised absence of black Africans; the strength of their unacknowledged collective presence living beneath the pervasive power of a colonial structure whose fast-transforming and more brutal meaning was yet to be acknowledged by the world at large: apartheid.

As a teenager none of this was clear to me, either analytically or politically. Loss, a large field in which new meanings lie submerged. Just the odd boulder from an African past, perhaps? A strong, quiet presence, hardly visible and only just felt, lying as though in the open land, a mass felt beneath the open palm of an uncertain young hand.

Early in my student years, I had an unexpected visit from Johannesburg architect and friend of my father since their immigrations to South Africa in the late-1930s. As a child, I had hardly known Erich Mauthner, but now we stood together on London's South Bank, him talking about the importance of modern town planning and me somewhat impatient at not understanding what all of this might be about. Underlying meanings seemed to swirl in the foggy air. Recently I came across Erich's name among those in Ernst May's group of young architects who worked, I now guess, with my father in Moscow. This also would have been around the time when Arthur Korn had met my grandfather, Bruno, in Der Ring in Berlin. So I now enjoy this small reassembly of events, bits scattered about across time by the force of the diaspora.

A common story, one among millions. But one whose influences impact on the architecture that we make? We all experience uncertainty, impermanence within the constant process of change, along with the affirmative sense of belonging. A fundamental ambivalence.

Such things weren't discussed among students or by our tutors. For, with the second world war over, hope, aspiration and the building of a modern world became the preface for the swing into the 1960s, as rock and roll's emerging youth culture began edging in to disturb the established patterns.

So why, at the end of my student days at the AA, did I feel the need to get away? Liz and I were married and expecting our first child, and I had a strong relationship with my two student friends (and partners-to-be), Richard and Paul, so why not stay and make it happen? Perhaps I felt a kind of

Left
Paul Koralek, Liz Ahrends, Peter Ahrends, John Donat and Mireille Burton, photographed by Richard Burton on a Bosphorus ferry as it passes Istanbul's Dolmabahce Palace.

restlessness? Where is home to be? I certainly felt a sense of loyalty to my distant parents, so the plan was to go back to Johannesburg and work for a year or two in my father's office before returning to London where we knew we wanted to make our lives.

In the event six of us – Richard and Mireille Burton, Paul Koralek, John Donat, Liz and I – travelled to the Middle East until Liz and I separated from the others and headed southwards on an oil tanker along the east coast of Africa to Capetown.

Why this journey of looping complexity across land and sea? I've long felt that paths of loopiness are a creative part of our inquisitive nature. In his essay 'Zigzagging' (published in 'Restless Cities', 2010), Mark Turner quotes from Le Corbusier's early book The City of Tomorrow: 'Man walks in a straight line because he has a goal and knows where he is going; he has made up his mind to reach some particular place and goes straight to it. The pack-donkey meanders along, meditates a little in his scatter-brained and distracted fashion, he zigzags in order to avoid the larger stones, or to ease the climb, or to gain a little shade; he takes the line of least resistance'. This description of alternative paths, contrasting the rational straight line with the unhurried meanderings of a donkey, suggests a disturbingly restrictive view – take one route or the other – rather than recognising the potential of both. Pack-donkey or not, I find myself drawn to the delightfully easy path of an occasional zigzag while also recognising, valuing and enjoying the straight line forward.

Our trip to Turkey and Persia – a great experience achieved with the unquestioning confidence of student energy – was certainly not a straight line. Liz and I decided to go to South Africa for a year or two before making a life together in London. Why not, she'd suggested, drive all the way through Africa? Yes, let's do it. We had no money, no jeep, no experience of overland treks, but we knew another young couple at the AA who might want to make the journey with us and, hopefully, help fund the jeep. Denise and Robert Scott Brown initially agreed but after some thought, probably quite sensibly, pulled out. An alternative plan was required.

For us, air travel was unaffordable, so why not choose the most obvious route, by sea from Southampton to Cape Town, as I'd been taken in 1937 at the age of three. Just too obvious, we felt, and what's to be experienced in a fortnight on a liner? In any case a loopy alternative was fast taking hold in discussions between the six of us involving a second-hand Land Rover with roll-down canvas sides (good, we thought, for summer travel), towing a tarpaulined two-wheel luggage trailer. We would head east through Europe to Turkey and eventually to Persia (now Iran). There Liz and I would peel off to the southern oil port of Khorramshahr to find a cheap passage on an oil tanker and make our way to South Africa. The other four planned to return to London in the autumn. As often seems to happen, a key part of our initial plan evaporated. A fellow student, the son of a shipping magnate, had offered to help. He had assured me that 'all was arranged' for the tanker journey, but on the eve of our departure his mother phoned to say it wasn't. We set off the following morning, unphased.

Two AA travel scholarships helped make the trip viable and provided an underlying academic purpose. Our mode of travel to what were regarded as remote areas was unusual, but it gave rise to an extraordinary variety and depth of experience as well as compelling insights into wholly unfamiliar cultures. Displaying little sense of formality or

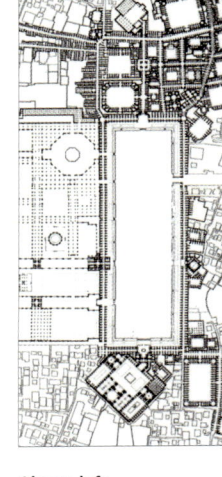

Above left
Ali Bakhtiar, Paul Koralek, Peter Ahrends, Liz Ahrends, Mireille Burton, Richard Burton and John Donat at Bakhtiar's house in Isfahan.

Above
Plan of Maidan Square and district in Isfahan; views of the covered bazaar, which leads off the square.

finesse, this group of enthusiastic students seemed to encourage an opening of doors and a trusting acceptance of our mission. Despite having almost no common language, we always felt welcomed.

Architecturally I was impressed not so much by the monumental structures we saw as the indigenous character of cities, towns and villages, and this appreciation later came to inform ABK's work. This influence is not obvious, however, because the process of absorption and integration has nothing to do with similitudes of representation or the reconstitution of the architectural languages of earlier and different cultures. We were young, modern architects. We rejected pastiche and were dismissive of the facile incorporation of historic motifs, a fatuous game that briefly prevailed in the 1980s when post-modernism was fashionable. Neither refinement nor innovation, we saw post-modernism as a failure of the human spirit and a digressive constraint of the imagination, a cultural pandemic that crossed the Atlantic, held sway for a decade or so, and then burnt itself out.

Arriving in Isfahan almost unannounced, these six student scruffs knocked on the door of Ali Bakhtiar, an AA-educated architect. In a spontaneous gesture of hospitality, he immediately offered to give over a good part of his inner-city house to us. We stayed for many weeks, making the central area of the city the focus of our studies.

We were drawn instinctively to Maidan Square, the remarkable mosques and palace, but it was above all the winding route of the covered bazaar that I found most compelling. This vivid alignment, memorably buzzing with the everyday qualities of market life, formed a stretched but containing route from which you'd come upon a variety of significant public

Above right
Pascal Coste's Place Royale et mosquée Masjid-i-Shah (1840), a depiction of Isfahan's Maidan Square (now Naqsh e Jahan Square) (ph: Monuments modernes de la Perse mesurés, dessinés et décrits, éd Morel, 1867).

Above
Maidan Square, the bazaar and mosque today.

places – an accommodation of the intense daily ordinariness of the city's well-being.

Markets carry this dynamic energy in our secular lives; in Europe they are often in a covered hall, near the edges of a square or simply formed by open stalls along a spreading set of streets. But in Isfahan the market was an enclosed route, a long string of variegated beads – brick vaults, spatial volumes in shaded daylight, cool in spite of the summer's heat. Geometrically this seemingly casual alignment formed its own thing rather than announcing what was to come next, whether mosques, caravanserai, public baths or lateral off-shoots between the matrix of houses grouped around unseen courtyards. It was the singular and fascinating power of this alignment, a well-peopled, active route, that etched itself into my mind as the city's primary architectural element.

Much of the land we crossed, moving from city to city, was plateau-like, scrubby but not quite a desert, and often ringed by distant mountains. In the summer, the dry sun-baked surface spread wide, encouraging dormant memories of similar South African landscapes to surface.

But look again. In the heat-hazed distance, small flecks of vivid green spoke of things growing, but not yet distinguishable was a mud-bricked village, announced by earth mounds denoting a linear route across the dry land. These underground freshwater canals (qanats) reached down from the distant mountain range to serve the plateau settlement – a different string of beads announcing the water-line. In the village of Natanz (destined to become a major nuclear facility), we saw straw-reinforced mud bricks being made and aligned in sweeping curves for sun-drying before being used by bricklayers to repair the mosque. Just a few people,

Above
Decorative detail from the Friday Mosque (latterly the Jameh Mosque).

Opposite
Peter Ahrends, Paul Koralek and Richard Burton, photographed by John Donat at Persepolis.

skilled in traditional techniques, transforming mud into bricks and then making domes, from the base to the apex, without the need for centering, with fluent low-key ease. In its decorated luminosity, the turquoise-tiled drum and dome expressed, in that remote place, the significance of Islam – message and architectural form establishing a clear and powerful unity.

Seeing the power of these hand-crafted forms, and appreciating the traditional mosque layouts and compositions (though ignorant of their religious content), I was drawn to their clarity. First, it seemed to be a story of exteriors and interiors, and sometimes the essential (and seemingly 'unfinished') qualities of the light, earth-coloured brick-built geometric masses in contrast to the laid-on colour-brightness of the decorated outer layer of faience tiles; intricate messages of stunning turquoise beauty. For this atheist-to-be these contrasts (earth and heaven?) were clear and powerful. Second, there was the functional meaning of the community-serving rectangular courtyard, an open gathering place set beside the intensity of the dome's religious interior focus. Together these two aspects seemed to offer an understanding of the value of a place of secular social assembly adjacent to the world of Islam.

Could it be that the language of architecture contains a sense of connectivity that lies beyond the specifics of any historic culture? In the ten years since the human genome was first mapped we've learned that the global spread of our genetic connections provides a binding sense of who we are as a species – so perhaps it wasn't surprising that these new cultural glimpses resonated in my young mind. The broad sweep of the Modern Movement in architecture, and within it the work of ABK, should not be thought of as either a representation or an exclusion of historic cultural strains; instead we'll consider different connections.

Driving across the Anatolian plain, the emptiness of the landscape seemed even more special in the absence of other vehicles. We were on our own, apart from the occasional road-hugging tortoises – fellow travellers, we thought, all heading in the same direction. Suddenly, around a hilly bend, we came across a strangely beautiful scene in the valley below – an eroded landscape of sandstone pinnacles. Washed away or broken down over time, these odd structures exposed signs of former habitation in their carved-out, cave-like interiors. We wondered what destructive force had been wreaked on this community, this Christian monastery of old. Down in the valley we came across a grove of untended apricot trees – remnants of an orchard stretching along the stream's gentle alignment.

About thirty years later I visited Beirut with a Palestinian friend to see the site of a competition for the city's new Souk. A local guide took us on an unofficial tour through the war-scarred streets, careful to avoid remaining landmines. The district was largely deserted, and we passed blocks of flats, their facades torn away but occasionally revealing signs of inhabitation. This conjunction of war-wrought violence and domestic belongings laid bare was disturbing, not least because it brought back images from the well-guarded recesses of my mind of the destroyed Anatolian monastery, as well as childhood photo memories of war-torn Berlin and London's Blitz, the aftermath of which was still evident when I arrived in 1951. Seen in relation to the central drive of my work – the making of architecture – I found these repetitions of city destruction disturbing.

ABK: Dialogue, Consultation and Collaboration

Much of ABK's work was for housing, education, health and civic buildings commissioned from the public sector. Wherever possible, within that framework and alongside the involvement of client and statutory bodies, we would seek to engage in a dialogue with the future occupants. This wasn't to focus on physical form but rather to consider what sort of a new place could be envisaged – what could it be like both internally and as an inhabited entity in the neighbouring context.

Two examples come to mind. The first is an unbuilt proposal from the early 1970s for a new headquarters building for the Post Office on a vacant site to the north of St Paul's Cathedral. While the overall architectural form has a relevance to the wider urban context, it was in consultations with the workforce (both management and unions) that the key themes of the project were developed. Our conceptual sketches showing the building set in its historic context filled our minds, and we suggested that, in the process of sharing design aspirations, we might also bring people together. Visiting comparable buildings in northern Europe, we ate and drank along the way, talking about the substance of our design. Ideas, described without the mystique of 'professionalism' became our shared commodity, and a consensus emerged that would have given rise to a distinctive modern building of interesting parts and ideas. But it wasn't to be. The day before the opening of a public exhibition that was being set up on the vacant site, the project fell victim to a round of sudden, severe spending cuts by Jim Callaghan's Labour government. Despite such setbacks, as architects we don't 'lose' ideas – they live on, emerging or attaching elsewhere, often with unexpected slants and refreshed meanings.

Right
Post Office headquarters, London (1975), model and typical floor plan. This unexecuted proposal, for an empty bombsite on St Martin's le-Grand, to the north of St Paul's Cathedral, comprised two segments of open-plan offices, separated by service cores, with a public route through the building connecting two ground-level landscaped areas. ABK's project was cancelled before it was due to start on site, and the headquarters was eventually built in 1984 to a nondescript design by ABK's original client, the Property Services Agency.

Left
Paul Koralek, Peter Ahrends and Richard Burton on the Poplar station bridge of the Docklands Light Railway.

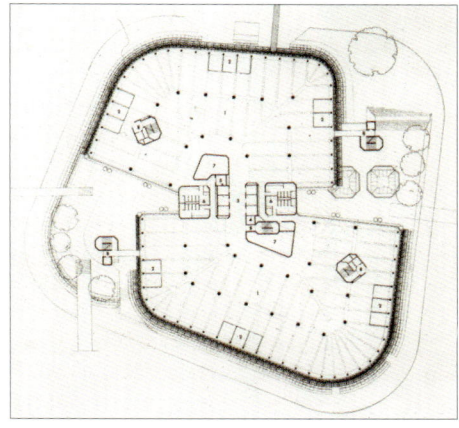

Some years later we undertook another complex, large-scale consultation with the workforce of Cummins, a well-established industrial enterprise in Scotland. Involving the factory's unions for day and night shifts (blue- and white-collar workers), the exercise was carried out with the enthusiastic authority of the company president and his colleagues at the American parent company. Based in the Central Lowlands community of Shotts, and manufacturing relatively small numbers of beautifully designed diesel engines, Cummins wanted to extend its plant at the greenfield edge of the town. We asked radical questions, enjoyed periods of unforeseen research, and blind alleys were followed by leaps of imagination. Underlying this probing design process, the dialogue of consultation with the workforce helped to suggest new directions for the design team. Given the strategy to expand the plant, what attitudes, we asked, might the different employees have to their place of work? What wish-list of priorities could form significant parts of the brief? By discussing ideas with the workforce during the design process might we find a sharing of ideas? Neither ownership patterns nor profits were discussed but rather ways and means of making a good place to work – an aspiration which, along with management's blue-sky thinking on several fronts (sustainability, the encouragement of a shared awareness of production and achievement, improved environmental controls such as dust, lighting and acoustics), shared a set of standards and, importantly, design ideas that were responsive to progressive ambitions.

But did these consultations and concerns for people-based issues influence the design? Yes, for by drawing attention to some of the environmental aspects that emerged, a discourse of many parts was achieved. This wasn't a box-ticking exercise where requests are satisfied by a corresponding provision. Instead recognition was given to the comments, from which a sub-set of parts was considered. To be more specific, the linear arrangement of the plan (whereby materials and parts are fed in at one end, and finished, tested engines emerge at the other) had been preferred by the client as a manufacturing sequence, and this was best served by a series of linked but discrete buildings forming workshops to accommodate a rational manufacturing process.

Alternative production arrangements were considered, always in response to the need to keep the factory operating while radical changes were being made on site. New buildings set the aesthetic of the whole complex while the altered existing ones would serve as repurposed elements within a much-expanded family of parts.

The Cummins project had a particularly satisfying outcome, both in terms of the overall functional arrangement of the plant and the care that was taken to enhance the wellbeing of the workforce.

Further examples give a brief and sketchy view of other applications of social enquiry applied to a large number of different buildings types by a productive response to clients' programmes.

Left
Cummins Engines Factory, Shotts, Lanarkshire (1975-83). 'This complex project was underpinned by a comprehensive consultation process', says Peter Ahrends. 'Covered ways from the car park link to the interface zones (containing people services) between adjacent workshops. Rather than the economically preferred convention of artificially-lit deep-plan manufacturing floors, we opted for bright spaces, with rooflights offering views of the changing Scottish skies. The external walls provide a series of bay windows (places for sandwiches, tea and cards at lunchtime), whose facetted geometry also help disperse noise in the workshops. The shared canteen overlooks the end-of-line assembled engines – manufactured beauties which everybody in the plant had a hand in making.'

Above
Chalvedon housing, Basidon (1968-77), a low-rise residential scheme punctuated by gardens and pedestrian routes on a 33-hectare site in the new town zone.

Right
Mendelsohn and Chermeyeff's De La Warr pavilion, Bexhill-on-Sea (1935); ABK's 2003 competition-winning proposal for an adjacent mixed-use development was approved in principle by the council but contested by residents.

In the late 1960s we planned a large area of housing in Chalvedon, Basildon, which was built in three phases. This allowed us to work with a social psychologist to survey, absorb and analyse the views of new occupants, and in turn make adjustments to the later phases. These were relatively early days in the now more common process of consultation – a progressive lesson showing how early intervention can serve as a means of interaction.

In more recent times we won a competition to plan a number of buildings intended to help regenerate Bexhill's seafront, adjacent to Erich Mendelsohn and Serge Chermayeff's iconic and much-admired De la Warr Pavillion (1935). Finding that Mendelsohn had himself designed an unbuilt project for a mid-height hotel beside the pavilion, our extended team consulted a variety of interest groups in the town. The initial response seemed positive, but not for long as residents mobilised to oppose this change. Retention of an existing pitch-and-putt space was deemed essential, and not to be altered by our modest, low-rise proposals designed to meet the Bexhill regeneration brief. Despite putting forward a compelling economic case, the scheme was subsequently withdrawn by our client.

Mendelsohn's drawings, depicting a large hotel on a site immediately adjacent to the Pavilion, display no evidence of timidity – the strength of client conviction is as essential, today, as it was in the 1930s. While respecting the local democratic process that rejected the scheme, there was a sense of frustration that the case for a new project that promised positive outcomes for Bexhill had been dismissed.

Much has been written about modern architecture's failure to blend quietly and positively with historic urban contexts. There's an assumption

that modern idioms speak too loudly, too brashly and uncaringly. Or is it that we feel disturbed and discomforted when faced with new intrusions?

A significant amount of ABK's work falls into this category – our assertion being that important modern interventions are designed to enhance the fabric of our cities, our towns and villages – including projects built and unbuilt, and of different types and materials. They share (though not idiomatically) our central commitment to make clear modern work amidst the well-loved fabric of historic urban areas – for it's a joy to be there, offering new notes and melodies.

In looking at these projects I recognise that we often come up against widely-held prejudice against modern architecture. When, in 1984, Prince Charles damned our competition-winning design for the National Gallery extension in Trafalgar Square, he seemed to strike a chord, at least in the UK media.

For several decades the National Gallery had hoped to build an extension on a vacant site at the north-west corner of the square. In line with Margaret Thatcher's politics of privatisation, a brief was prepared by the Property Services Agency (PSA) inviting developers to submit applications in a limited competition with their chosen architects. The gallery's space requirement was to be met in conjunction with office space that would be leased to the developer. In commercial terms, this represented a mixed-use development in which the gallery extension would piggy-back on the offices below, producing an expressed concern at the prospect of market forces being used to procure an extension to one of the world's great art galleries.

Six developer-led teams were selected and we were pleased to be appointed by Trafalgar House, who we found appreciative of our design ideas for

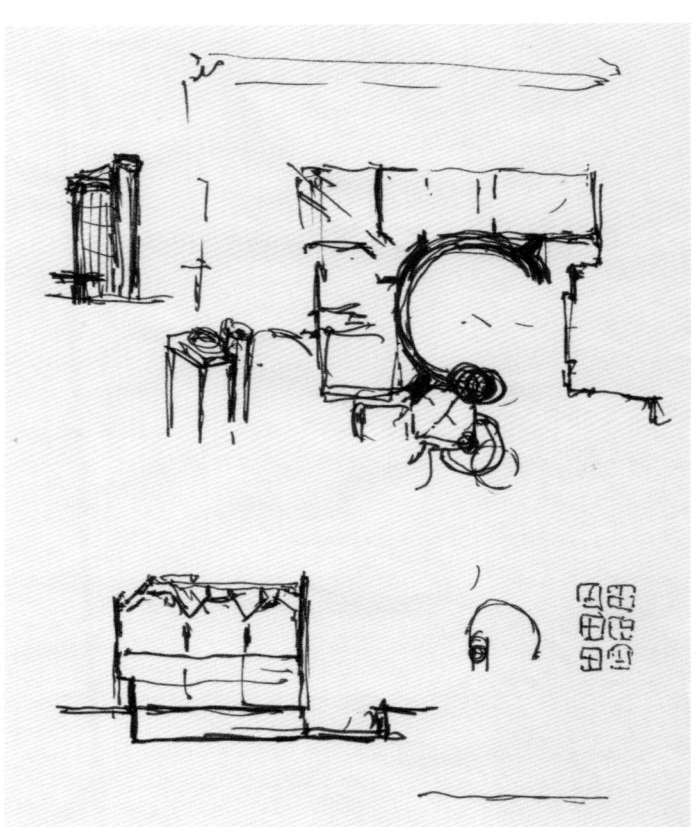

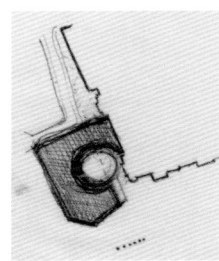

Above/right
ABK's first scheme for the National Gallery extension (1982), won in a developer-led competition. The new building on the Hampton site at the corner of Trafalgar Square was to include a significant proportion of office space to help fund the galleries.

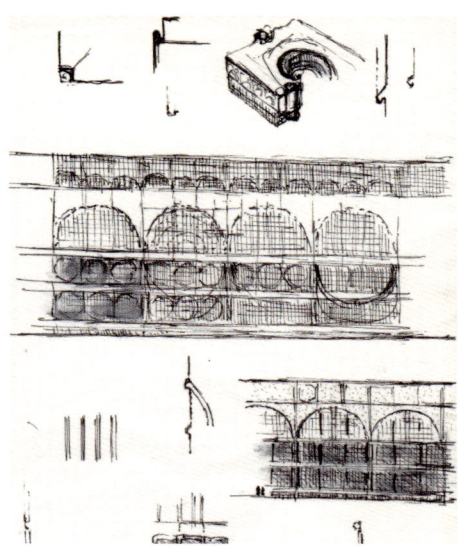

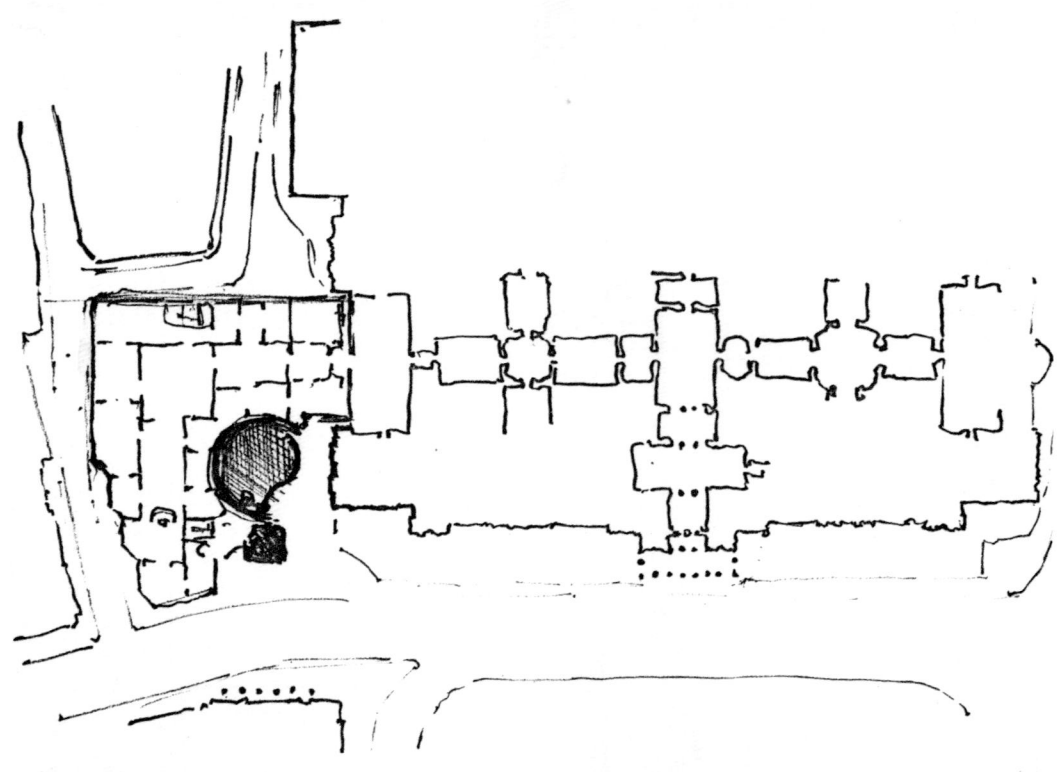

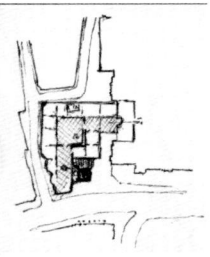

Left/right
Revised in collaboration with the National Gallery, ABK's second scheme (1983) increased the total floor space at the expense of the dimensions of the central court, while also adding a glazed tower, topped by a cafe, which marked the entrance to the new galleries.

an unusual arrangement of galleries to house the Early Renaissance collection. Externally, our scheme centred on a circular court, celebrating the on-site public realm by forming a new pedestrian link towards Leicester Square. The arrangement was intended to make a clear and relatively modest overall building mass, providing the required space for the gallery and offices, but no more. The court was to have generous proportions, and establish a well-articulated, lively relationship with the west facade of the gallery.

The competition submissions were exhibited, and visitors were invited to rate the designs by a point-scoring method. While this was probably not the most significant factor for the assessors, it may have helped tip the selection in our favour.

Architectural competitions can have messy aftermaths, and that was certainly the case here. At the initial meeting with the gallery trustees and their PSA advisors it became evident that they wanted to review aspects of our design. Would we be willing to work with the director to take on board their views? Of course, I replied, not knowing that the trustees, in the light of some of the other entries, were keen to achieve more floor space, with a consequent effect upon the office provision.

Travelling abroad with the National Gallery staff to view their preferred exemplars, I soon understood that their values were conventional and, not surprisingly, they were hungry for space. With hindsight it became clear that these demands brought pressure to bear on the viability of the mixed-use formula, and so compromised the conceptual basis of our design.

With the to-ing and fro-ings of a protracted design review, ructions became evident amongst some of the trustees, but eventually they approved our revised

design. A planning application was submitted to Westminster Council which, unsurprisingly, was called in for a public inquiry. Lord Annan, chairman of the National Gallery's trustees, and its director Sir Michael Levey gave their support. The subsequent planning inspector's report was interpreted as favourable, albeit with minor reservations, and our client was advised to expect a positive outcome from the Secretary of State.

But this was not to be, for soon came an intervention by Prince Charles, who had been invited by the RIBA to present the 1984 Royal Gold Medal to the celebrated Indian architect Charles Correa at Hampton Court Palace. As part of his wider mission to trash modern architecture, Charles took the opportunity to severely criticise and, in effect, damn our design for the National Gallery.

By chance I had arranged an early morning meeting with Trafalgar House on the following day. First thing, over coffee, they said that Charles had killed the scheme. They were right. Patrick Jenkin, Secretary of State for the Environment, went against the reported view of the planning inspector and refused planning permission.

So it was that Prince Charles, in the first of his anti-modern speeches, could do no better than give voice to a vilification, a view that seemed to know no better and see no further than a deep-seated conservatism. There was no analysis of our proposal, nor recognition of the value of urban gestures, such as the circular mini-court that we envisaged as a modern echo of the defined place and geometry of the nearby Admiralty Arch, to form a new and tightly-scaled antechamber at this north-west corner of Trafalgar Square. The intention was to make places, routes and formal masses that offered new urban connections and meanings. Rather, we were attacked with a mindless catchphrase language of mean epithets abundant with images of 'carbuncles', 'glass stumps', and 'fire-station towers'.

Asked how he composed music Beethoven is said to have responded: 'I hear the sounds in my head and write them down until they stop'. The often unspoken process of making a design is perhaps not dissimilar. My preference is to tread lightly, like the honey bee, collecting and connecting ideas as we make marks on the pages of urbanism.

Back in 1964, as a young practice we had looked at a war-damaged site in Soho, about half a mile north of the National Gallery. The progressive vicar of St Anne's Church had invited us to design a modern church and its adjunct as part of a new group of buildings to include Samuel Pepys Cockerell's early-nineteenth-century bell tower, a finely shaped beacon that had survived the Blitz bombing that destroyed the church. The project, to be funded by a multi-storey underground car park beneath the new ensemble, was to comprise a tightly-grouped, finely chiselled set of forms offering a dense new urban story, a diaphanous skin (an invented translucence of layers of glass and perforated metal) unifying the crystalline elements of the whole. Distinctive but not grandiose, and contributing a vibrant new particle to Soho's urban grain, the design still speaks to me half a century later as a labour of love.

So why no building? Not unusually, the funding didn't work out. But strong ideas are seldom lost and, as if stirred by an unseen force into the fertile gene pool of the Modern Movement, often seem to emerge in later projects.

About ten years afterwards ABK designed a new building for Keble College in Oxford, which was built in two phases. Our scheme related to William

Right
St Anne's Church redevelopment, Soho (1964). The church tower, which survived wartime bombing, was to be joined by a new church hall and associated facilities, all clad in a translucent glazed skin.

Left
Peter Ahrends' sketches for the second National Gallery scheme.

Butterfield's Gothic Revival college buildings which so strikingly (but not, to my mind, warmly) occupied the whole urban block, except for our one remaining corner site. With the richness of his decorated red-brick structures, Butterfield made a bold move away from the honey-coloured stone facades of earlier Oxford college quads. And his planning of the student room buildings (accessed from a central corridor rather than by staircase to 'sets' of rooms) also broke radically with tradition. So why suggest that these differences have importance? Most obviously the phrase 'red-brick university' isn't associated with Oxbridge. And similarly, the central corridors serving a large number of rooms also carry a different social significance to the more exclusive sets.

Does ABK's design, with its formal and massing characteristics and the use of contrasting glass and brick on the inner and outer facades respectively, create a world so different from Butterfield's idiom as to be seemingly without respect for his expressive statement? On the contrary – that would be a superficial reading which even the non-conformist Butterfield might have challenged.

The aesthetic dimensions opened up by the Modern Movement paved the way for radical opportunities. In the case of our work at Keble, consider the significance of being able to make contrasting 'external' and 'internal' facades, with a subtle interplay between hard-edged straight-line masonry masses and the taut skin of cascading glass curvatures. As to respecting Butterfield's work, the new building steps down in height as its curved alignment approaches and modestly passes the impressive mass and historic splendour of the college's central hall and library building.

Left
Student residential accommodation, Keble College, Oxford (1972-80). Conceived as a curved and containing wall comprising brick on the street side and extensive glazing facing inwards to the college, the student rooms thereby looked both to the city and introspectively to academia.

Here you'll find conversations about the importance of independence between old and new in a spirit of architectural togetherness – conceptually, both are equally energetic, the distinction marked by clarity rather than aggression.

How do these values relate to the work that the practice carried out for the Nebenzahl house on the southern edge of the old city of Jerusalem, a historic environment of a very different kind?

There were many contributing factors in the project: culture, politics, religion and not least a stunningly beautiful site at the war-torn end of a line of historic buildings within the city wall. Here, in the Jewish quarter, our deeply religious client wanted to gain unrestricted views from the upper level of his family house to the Wailing Wall. Southwards, across the city wall to the Palestinian sector of East Jerusalem in the valley below, lay the beautiful historic landscape of Kidron. There was no inkling in my untutored mind of the political scenario that was later to unfurl with the widespread construction of Israeli settlements in the Occupied Territories.

Facing the site from the balcony of a rather basic hotel lying in the Palestinian part of valley below in East Jerusalem, we ranged across sets of ideas, putting aside our initial interlocking Cubist-like ideas in favour of the simple strength of a street-aligned wall raised above the new datum of an open, raised entrance place.

But how should we make this wall? While taking a meandering walk through the neighbouring historic district (which, I later learned, was the Mount of Olives), the seemingly contradictory idea of a stone curtain emerged. This element would comprise a single unifying plane, given its energy and life by an individuation and displacement of window patterns; each element serving the plan's interior

arrangement, floor-by-floor, and contained by a termination of the building's 'free' end. This established a means of turning the corner and completing the wall's pattern-story, while – with our client in mind – being a celebration of and orientation towards the Wailing Wall.

Also in mind was the stone-wall facade of Oxford's original Bodleian Library which, when I first saw it, evoked a kind of lightness, in spite of its evident opaque mass. Another thought relates to the house-plan type, an outward-looking orientation extending from back to front along its length. In this arrangement the street facade wall occupies a special place, mediating between the interior life of the house and the expansive historic world that lies beyond. This fascination with the qualities of back and front, inside and outside, recurs in different expressions elsewhere in our work.

Above
The Nebenzahl House, Jerusalem (1968-72). Located adjacent to the old city walls, the stone house was designed by ABK for Yitzhak Ernst Nebenzahl (1907-92), then State Comptroller of Israel, and his wife. The principal residence occupied the top level, and much attention was given to views of the nearby Wailing Wall. Two flats for other members of their orthodox family and a guest flat were situated on lower floors.

Gathering Places

Many of ABK's schemes are characterised by enclosed external gathering spaces: courts, quads and forecourts, both public and private. Most also have spatial and material qualities that are associated with an appreciation of the architecture of the surrounding buildings.

At Trinity College, Dublin, the library forecourt consists of a raised podium that establishes a new type of open place within the college, set between two historic buildings, the new library and three adjacent open spaces.

There was a particular focus on places at Chichester Theological College, where a new pedestrian route was established between the existing chapel and the historic central building as well as the open access routes formed within the new building's cross movements.

In contrast, at Grenoble, the masterplan envisaged occupying and inhabiting the open space between existing roads (a central axis), thereby forming a variety of gathering places between new buildings to establish a dense new urban spine. This identifiable people-orientated city fragment is set amidst the spacious greenery of the suburban character of the existing campus.

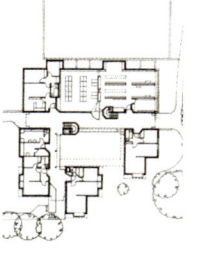

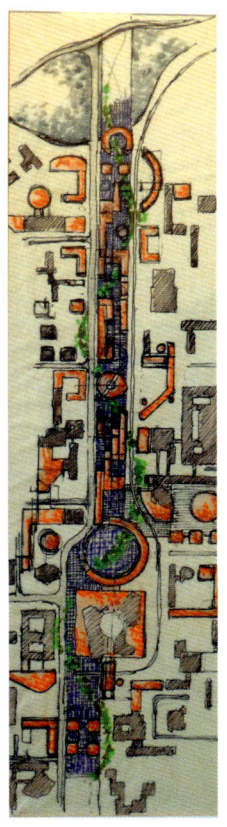

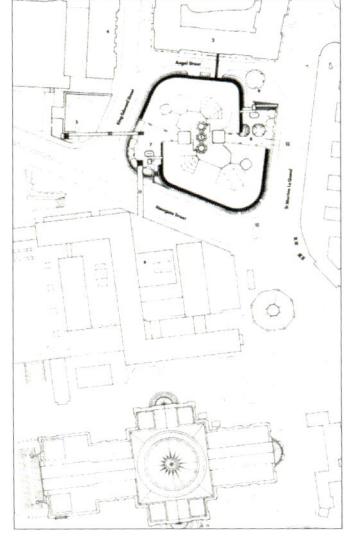

Above
Masterplan for Grenoble University (1990). The tight new urban spine gives form and intensity to the otherwise 'suburban' plan of the 1960s campus.

Right
Perspective and plan, Post Office headquarters (1975); main hall and playground, Eastfield School, Thurmaston (1968).

Left
Forecourt at Berkeley Library, Trinity College Dublin (1961-67); glazed mini quad and bar interior at Keble College, Oxford (1972-80); Chichester Theological College – the route and court (1961-65).

Clusters and Groupings

In some of ABK's projects, the brief and design process gave rise to a set of buildings which together contribute to the sense of a larger whole. In that way each component building retains its individuality without giving rise to full independence.

The unbuilt design for St Anne's Church in London's Soho brought together a range of elements, major and minor. None were quite detached, apart from the church tower that had survived wartime bombing and would now stand strong beside its newly adopted modern family – a welcome adjacency. Our intention was to embrace a radical set of modern ideas, and propose a different kind of urban statement in which elements form a cluster rather than a singular body.

At Hooke Park in Dorset, John Makepeace asked us to prepare a masterplan for a new furniture design college in which we were to consider the structural use of green wood forest thinnings. We developed three building types – a workshop, student residential rooms and a public building for visitors – each of which exploited a different structural form, but together making a coherent new settlement within a wooded glade. While the workshop and a prototype fragment of the residential buildings were built, the rest of the development plan remained uncompleted at the time. Working with the celebrated German architect and engineer Frei Otto, however, we were able to explore 'green' ideas, pioneering new fields of timber technology.

With the grand riverside site in Moscow, where we built the new British Embassy, the complexity was of another order. This was a story of four street-aligned elements, functionally and formally individuated, yet identifiably of the same civic family.

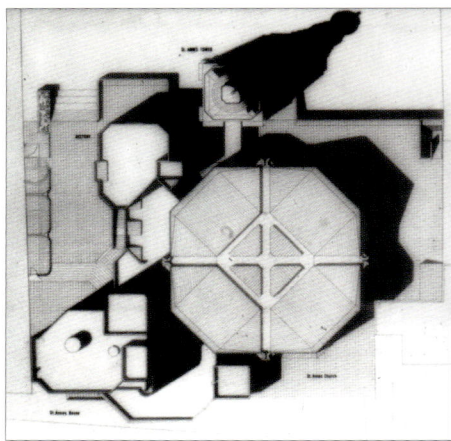

Above
Workshop interior and masterplan model, Hooke Park (1983-90); roof plan, St Anne's Church, Soho (1964).

Right
The British Embassy in Moscow (1988-2000) was conceived as a 'family' of buildings along the river front.

Entrances

The language of the Modern Movement lacked the traditional motifs for doorways that enrich classical architecture, and modern architects often fell short in creating convincing entrance solutions.

With the Berkeley Library at Trinity College Dublin, the approach to the entrance was marked by a generous flight of steps rising up to a paved urban space set between the facades of the adjacent historic buildings and the new one. In urban terms, we wanted to provide an intermediate outside 'room' which had a role within the hierarchy of college quads, while drawing visitors to the entrance doors by a series of set-backs in the new facade.

The arrangement and form of the building masses encourage entry as visitors step up to this level among the range of open spaces in the campus. The space was unique on the campus as a partly-differentiated mini-quad, but not as an entrance place. For, in the main quad, steps also rise to the grand portico of to the historic College Hall, a gathering and dining place of great distinction. And although our architectural approach with the library was not a conscious reference to this elevated tradition, there is a compatability in that they serve, on the one hand to provide fine food in the company of others, and on the other, books and knowledge. Both are wholesome ingredients of higher education – two aspects of sustenance, two architectures, two centuries apart. ABK went on to design other buildings at Trinity, and we participated in competitions for several major projects on the campus, but those we didn't win.

The Arts Faculty Building at Trinity was initially designed within the framework of a limited competition in 1976, for a boundary site then known and functioning as the Fellows' Garden. The new entrance was from a generous ramp from the quad which, significantly, formed a new public route into the college from Nassau Street (and the city beyond), opening up the previously closed southern boundary. Important as we felt this to be then, we didn't foresee the future tourist influx to the college from the long line of parked coaches on Nassau Street. Paul, who regarded this as the most significant move that we made at the college in our 30 years of involvement, might also agree that we

Above
A series of raised walkways link the parking areas with the workshops at Cummins Engines, Shotts, Lanarkshire (1975-83).

Right
The perimeter wall leads round to the gateway at the British Embassy in Moscow (1988-2000).

Left
Stairs lead up to the raised podium and entrance marked by set-backs in the facade at Berkeley Library, Trinity College Dublin (1961-67); a ramped public route forms an entrance to the Arts Faculty Building at TCD (1968-2003).

contributed three differently memorable buildings over these years. A privilege, we felt, to have worked with a remarkably receptive and forward-looking group of academics.

At the Cummins Engine plant in Shotts, we made a series entrances to the adjacent workshops along the quarter-mile length of the new factory building; three from the staff car park and a fourth to also serve visitors. The various process parts of the building provided the opportunity to make something special of their seams as people-related areas, with active linkages extending out towards the car park. This is little different in principle from a set of paths leading to the front doors of a terrace of houses. Here, given the scale of the open and often weather-beaten site, the covered ways served as sheltered entrance markers.

So in many of ABK's designs this focus on an internal route, concourse or street, is not only a primary ordering element within the plan but it is also linked with the many meanings of 'entrance'. The dynamic life of the bazaar in Isfahan and London's Victorian shopping arcades serve as powerful antecedents, offering a collective city-wide spatial order whose underlying meanings remind us of the inter-relationship between city and house, public/private elements of an urban whole.

Internal Routes

Many ABK projects, though different in type and form, incorporate routes that generate an underlying structure within the plan by introducing a focussed animation of people in their movement through space and place.

Cummins is discussed earlier but we should also look at the generous interior concourse at TCD Arts, the diagonal route running alongside the square grid-plan structures of the WH Smith offices, the sinuous covered garden route at Keble, and the quadrant form of the internal street at St Mary's Hospital on the Isle of Wight. In the unbuilt design for the Mary Rose Museum, a more complex set of movement-alignments responds to the history of the battle-torn ship that lay buried for centuries in the silt bed of the Solent.

In these projects we explored our interest in the overlappings of social interaction evident in urban 'threads', such as bazaars and arcades. Open-ended yet somewhat attached, these linear enclosures offer a variety of displayed goodies along with the characteristic dynamic inherent in the patterns of people movement: go straight, pause unexpectedly, meander, meet, watch people as they go by, drink coffee, reflect, and go back.

The latent energies of these archetypal enclosures found fitting places in some of our work. In our proposal for the National Gallery extension, for example, we designed a long gallery as an inner arc to contain a series of beautiful Early Renaissance paintings. While this was far removed from a bazaar, it could have evoked something of the same atmosphere and experience of juxtapositions in the gentle movement as you walked through the gallery.

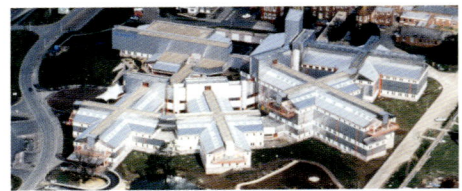
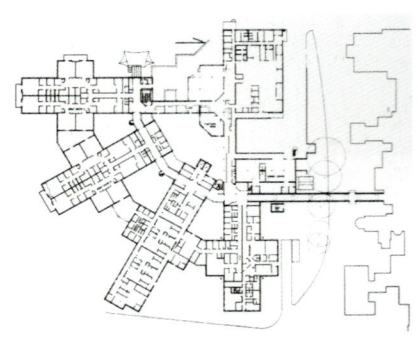

Left
Meandering walkway through Keble College Oxford (1972-80); the double-height concourse at TCD Arts Faculty building provides access to the wide variety of functions and routes; internal routes interconnect the cruciform plan blocks of St Mary's Hospital, Isle of Wight (1982-90).

Above
Sketch plan for WH Smith's headquarters (1982-85).

Right
Planning study for Leven Roaf, beside the River Lea in London's Tower Hamlets, considering street alignments as linear concourses lying beneath multi-storey urban spines (2004). Peter Ahrends' early sketch section for the proposed Mary Rose Museum (1980), exploring the relationship between the museum's parts and the main public route.

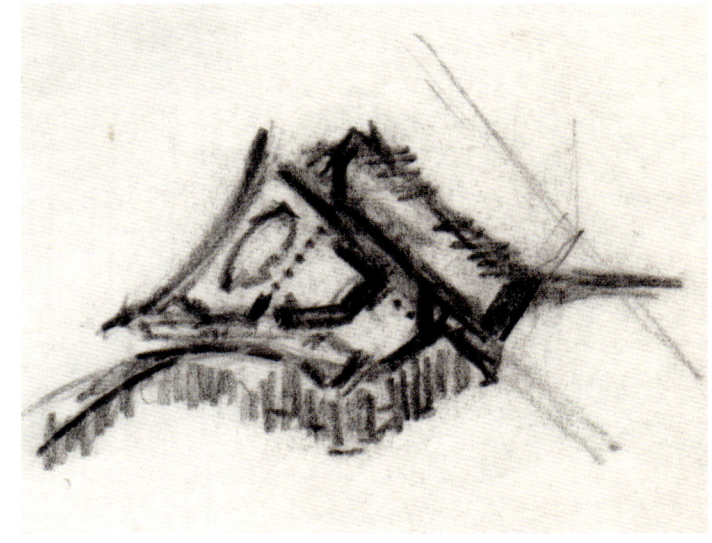

Two-Sidedness

Some of ABK's buildings express a difference of idiom and materiality between one face and another. This isn't just about the obvious differences between, say, front and back, public and private, or north and south orientations, although any one of these may also count.

At both Keble and TCD Arts, the new buildings occupy boundary sites within a quadrangled university – cloistered worlds separated from the street life of Oxford and Dublin respectively. This was evident at TCD where the stone boundary wall along Nassau Street defined the southern edge of what was then the Fellows Garden, a fine but underused green space with privileged access for the few. During the early stages of the design for Keble we considered the possibility of forming pedestrian access openings along the length of the main street boundary, but the college didn't regard this as a good idea. With both projects we developed the notion of a perimeter wall of masonry with relatively few window openings. Or, put another way, a hard-edged outer boundary wall expressing different 'orientations' to life inside and out.

In earlier work for the newly-established Templeton College on a greenfield site well outside Oxford's city limits, we designed a similar expression of two-sidedness (albeit not using masonry walls) for the residential accommodation. So, this set of ideas – an adoption/adaptation of 'college perimeter walls' – was also applied to ABK's design for a beautifully open rural site carrying no such urban precedents.

We were of a mind in thinking that there's more than one contextual reference behind these formal interpretations. At Templeton College we had prepared a masterplan in which the zigzags of the residential edge-buildings were differentiated from a diagonal axis that organised a continuum of lower buildings, including the library, teaching rooms, dining and other communal spaces – an interactively-layered story, and a modern one in which a reciprocal dialogue between building typologies was given a formal voice. The two sets of accommodation were separated by the intervening open spaces that were envisaged not as quads but rather a landscape that, by its enclosure, still carried

Left
An articulated masonry rear elevation and glazed, linear front at the Bryan-Brown House, Thurlestone Devon (1961). Keble College, Oxford (1972-80); the outer wall of brickwork with few openings hooks round to form and contain the mini-quad, whose contrasting fully-glazed inner wall splays outwards to shelter the garden walkway.

Right
The curved rear elevation contrasts with the more formal vertical street facade at the proposed office building on Shaftesbury Avenue, London (1986).

a resonance with the traditional collegiate form.

The Bryan-Brown House in Devon (1959-60) is an early example of two-sidedness. The linear plan had a southerly orientation towards the sea, while the masonry back may seem like something of a denial of an alternative, uphill northerly visual connection. Nor had we then felt the need to be more rigorous in following through with the meanings of the expressed materiality of this two-part arrangement. Had we been more thoroughly consistent, the whole back (with somewhat tower-like associations forming a set of white rendered enclosures) might have been more clearly differentiated from, say, a solely timber and glass front.

In principle, this is what we came to a decade later at Templeton College and Keble, but in a more definitive manner. Further examples of this ongoing preoccupation include the Nebenzahl House, Dunstan Road houses, Felmore housing, and the unbuilt projects for the British Telecom headquarters and the Shaftesbury Avenue offices.

Our proposal for the display of the Mary Rose contained half of the Tudor warship's hull and decks. Beside the resurrected vessel we formed curving edges to several levels of exhibition galleries in mirror-image and three-dimensional form, suggesting a delineation of the hull's missing port side. Spatially this intended ambiguity expressed the absence while more abstractly suggesting the presence of the ship's original whole.

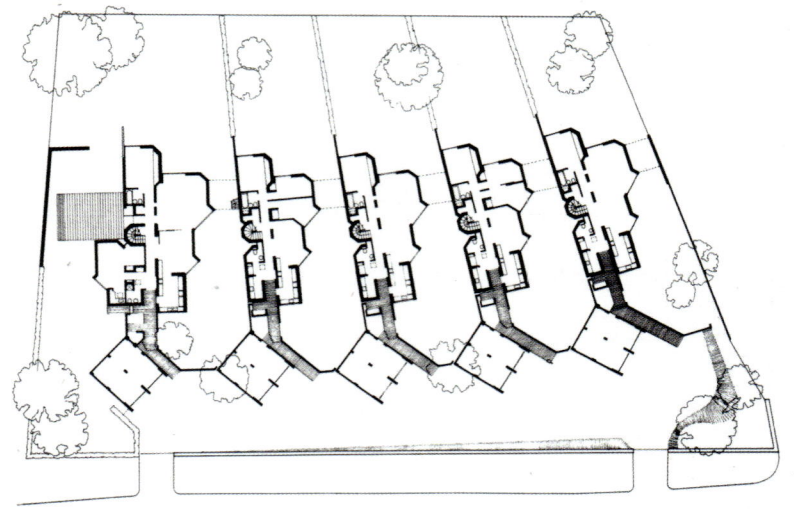

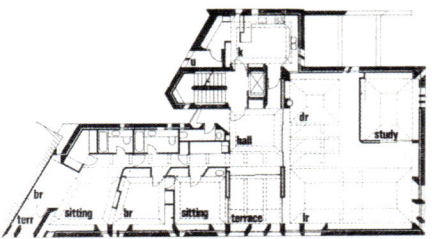

Above, left
The flank 'back' walls of the Dunstan Road houses in Headington (1966-69) form long party-wall baselines, providing privacy and containment in the sun-filled gardens. Templeton College near Oxford (1969-90); in contrast to the range of two-storey teaching buildings, the residential buildings form an outer edge to the gardens with a face of zinc-clad walls clearly differentiated from the fully-glazed inner wall. Nebenzahl house plan (1968-72), with living spaces arranged along the two 'outer' walls with views over the city.

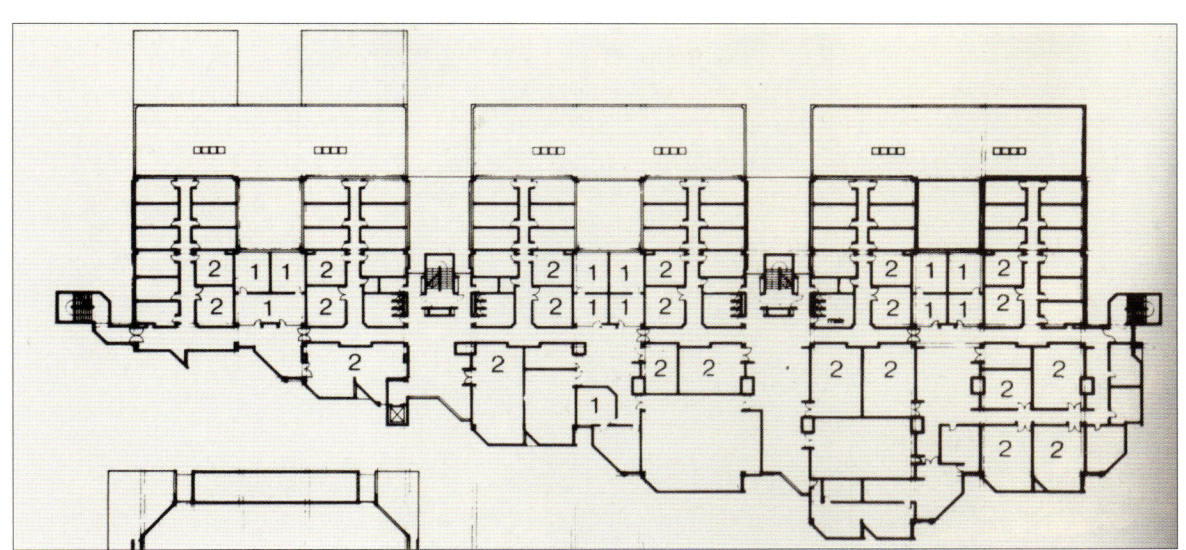

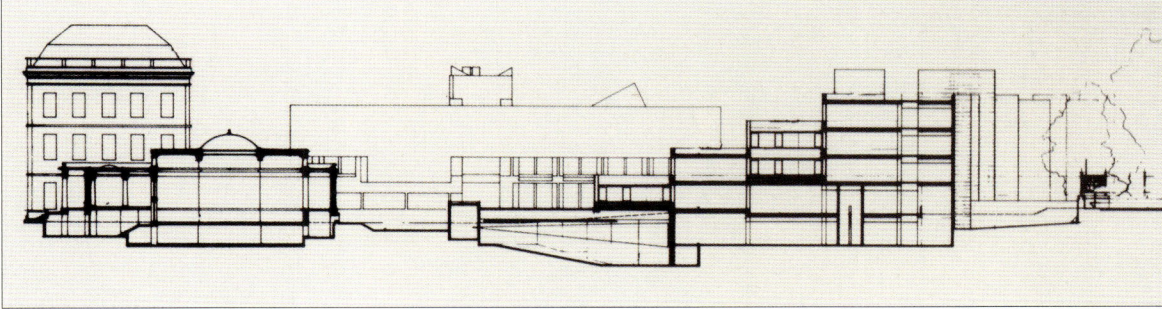

Right
An articulated street elevation of masonry walls with few openings contrasts with a repetitive tripartite massing at the inner face of the Arts Faculty at Trinity College Dublin (1968-2003), shown at upper level and in cross section.

Four-Square Buildings

In contrast to those projects which express underlying formal dualities, other ABK works are composed as freestanding rectangular buildings that sit confidently in their place.

At the Berkeley Library, the roof-lit reading room provides a spatial centre of gravity to the four-walled delineation of the plan, but the building's conceptual arrangement is actually somewhat asymmetric and complex in its sectional figuration, its engagement with adjacent buildings, and the orientations of pedestrian movement through college quads and adjacent open spaces.

Earlier I discussed the raised level of the library's entrance court, formed above a double-height basement of 'closed' library stacks and providing a largely unseen link to the old library's East Pavilion. In longitudinal section this forms a seemingly unexpressed L-shape, which by the spatial displacement of one element above the other establishes the library's entrance court, enabling diagonal pedestrian cross movements connecting three adjacent open spaces.

I first experienced this kind of spatial configuration in a remarkable village we happened upon as we travelled across Turkey's Anatolian Plain on route to Iran in the mid-1950s. Walls, flat roofs and open paved areas were all surfaced with straw-reinforced, sun-baked hard mud. This seemingly undifferentiated materiality offered pedestrian access, rising across one set of cubic formations onto the roofs of others – we felt like outsiders as we unwittingly stepped from the public spaces onto the roofs of adjacent private houses. This connectedness of materiality, surface and place offered a viewpoint from which the eye could roam and appreciate the sensory qualities of this remarkable community.

While Maidenhead Library is far removed from a remote village in Anatolia, here a spatial and formal unity is expressed by an independently structured space-frame roof overhanging the more complex forms at the plan's perimeter. Internally the unity of the double-height volume, the insertion of the mezzanine reference library, and the subtle zonings of various parts of the library service, together introduce an asymmetricising dynamic. A number of bay-like structures (internal alcoves with different

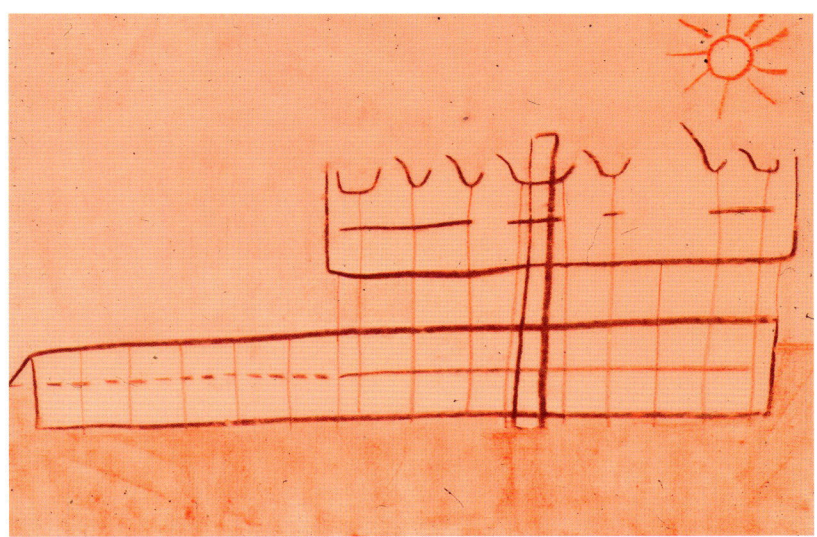

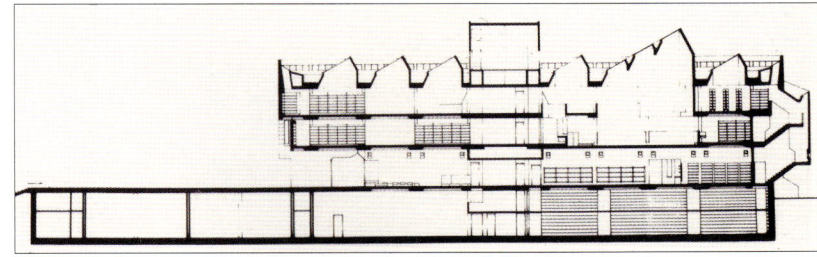

Above/left
The overtly simple four-square plan of the Berkeley Library at Trinity College Dublin (1961-67) belies its internal complexity and its functional/formal weighting in favour of the off-centre reading room. A different symmetry is evident in the longitudinal section, showing the extensive double-height closed stack in the raised basement.

Left
The square plan of Maidenhead Library (1966-73), reinforced by its overhanging space-frame roof, embraces a distinctly asymmetric arrangement of spaces (for instance the childrens' library and music library), which are expressed in the elevational composition.

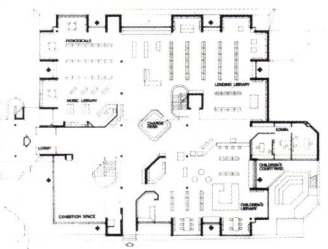

identities) reflects a set of functionally determined asymmetries – a dynamic describing the spatial meaning of the library's parts and their places in the balanced whole.

In the early 1970s we built two adjacent out-of-town low-cost buildings for Terence Conran during the early period of design retailer Habitat's extraordinary success. The project, near Wallingford, sought to bring effectiveness and clarity to the site with a language of simplicity and quiet, strong, formal moves. There are two sheds: the larger is a warehouse with mezzanine offices (the brilliant green external colour referenced Terence's Porsche), while the smaller building, a glazed and white-coloured showroom, displayed and sold the goodies stored in the adjacent warehouse stacks. Between these two rectangles we made a childrens' play area (for which Eduardo Paolozzi made climbing sculptures), toying with the idea of including a small glazed area to give glancing views into the big shed – sadly this never materialised.

So, does the concept of 'bay' have a wider meaning within the language of ABK's work? Without question; when we come to consider characteristic examples of the ways in which walls and roofs were designed, given form in our work, we'll explore those meanings in some depth.

Left
Offaly Civic Offices (1999-2002); the simplicity of the glazed rectangular office plan, set in a fine garden, was moderated and given a natural depth by an outer layer of timber trellis that served as a sun screen.

Above
The two buildings for Habitat in Wallingford (1972-74) contain respectively warehousing (with offices) and showroom facilities. A childrens' play area was provided beside the entrance with sculptural climbing structures made by Eduardo Paolozzi.

Squared Cross Grids

The square grid offers opportunities for a plan in which the occupation of different areas of enclosed space is served by adjacent courtyards, providing light, air and a localising landscaped identity. This planning device, first applied in our design for the Arts Faculty Building at Trinity College (and subsequently in a variety of unbuilt schemes), also served as a basis for the Regional Headquarters for WH Smith in Swindon.

By the late 1960s there were several modern precedents for applications of a square planning grid. For me the most important was Candilis, Josic & Woods' masterplan, part realised, for the Free University of Berlin – a novel interpretation of traditional Middle-Eastern low-rise courtyard housing like those we had seen on our study trip to Turkey and Iran in 1956. It is precisely these urban structures (such as at Isfahan), consisting of notable open spaces, a vibrant life along the covered route of the bazaar, and a matrix of low-rise courtyard houses, that echoed across time and space to offer a condensed new life in our designs.

But is it meaningful or even appropriate to compare major components from historic cities located in culturally different regions with my readings of ABK's work? If it provides insight into this late-in-life view, crossing time, culture, place and idiom, then yes.

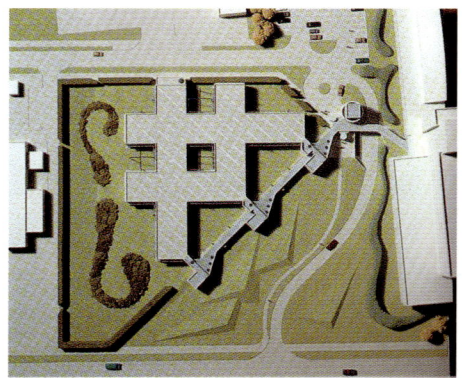

Right
British Airports Authority headquarters (1977). This competition entry for BAA's new complex at Gatwick Airport was an early example of ABK's deep-plan, cross-gridded layouts, bringing natural light and ventilation into the depth of the plan.

Left above
Arts Faculty, Trinity College, Dublin (1968-2003). Through the complex configuration of courtyards, a cross-gridded layout, a stepped section and the inward-facing orientation towards the newly-formed quad, sun, light and air were brought into the upper levels of the deep-plan faculty building.

Left below
WH Smith regional headquarters (1982-85); in contrast to the adjacent 1960s multi-storey block, we made a low, spreading garden building in which the two storey cross-gridded arrangement formed an even matrix of offices and landscaped courtyards. The second phase, not shown here, occupied the remainder of the triangular site.

Walls and Roofs

ABK's submission for the 1968 Canberra Bell Tower competition proposed a monument without walls. Instead a pair of curved lattice shells would have wall-like associations, but as diaphanous skins rather than opaque barriers. These independent elements were linked by an access core and, high up, the bells were contained within a pod. Symbolically the curvature of the structures suggested fragments of the earth's surface, while their conjunction might represent the shared histories of the UK and Australia. Strong, light, and dynamic, the project was intended to challenge conventions in proposing a new type of monument.

The curvature of plan forms, lattices and their geometrical triangulations recur in different marks and gestures in some of our later work, for instance at Keble, the Post Office headquarters and, later, the Mary Rose Museum.

Here too we find underlying binaries. We've touched on the influence of these characteristics in our work; manifestations of 'presence' and 'absence', powerful images such as the double-helix structure of DNA or political oppositions of 'left' and 'right' – ever present but unresolved.

While theoretical, ideological and material matters are influential in the process of design, my view is that in the initial analysis of a brief, we are touched by unforeseen factors that influence the direction we move in, each bringing energy to the emerging flow of ideas.

Describing our proposal for this unconventional bell tower, set on a small island in Lake Burley Griffin in the Australian capital, makes me realise the value of the latent energy of unrealised ideas, hanging in and occasionally stirring other bits of the mind's archive, a treasure chest of goodies. A distraction from a discussion of walls and roofs, perhaps, but it feels good to be living with a family of ideas, whether fulfilled or not.

Moving on, ranging across the various enclosing fabrics of ABK's work, it seems pertinent to return to the idea of the bay, noting its recurrence in several projects. While not a mainstream feature, it's one that carries a focussed meaning, shifting and adapting in its application, project by project.

By 'bay', I mean the natural form of a coastal bay,

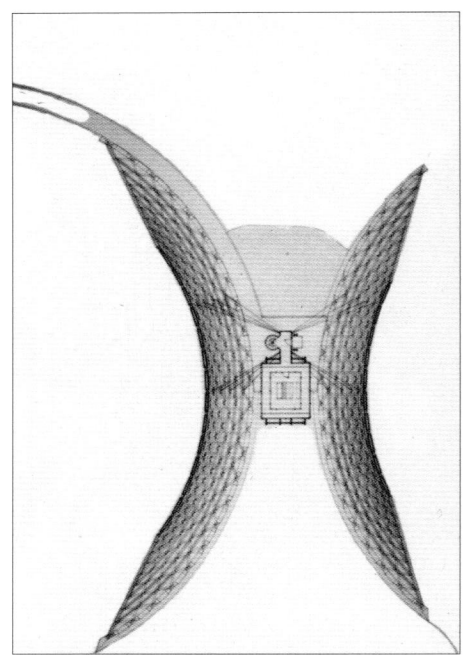

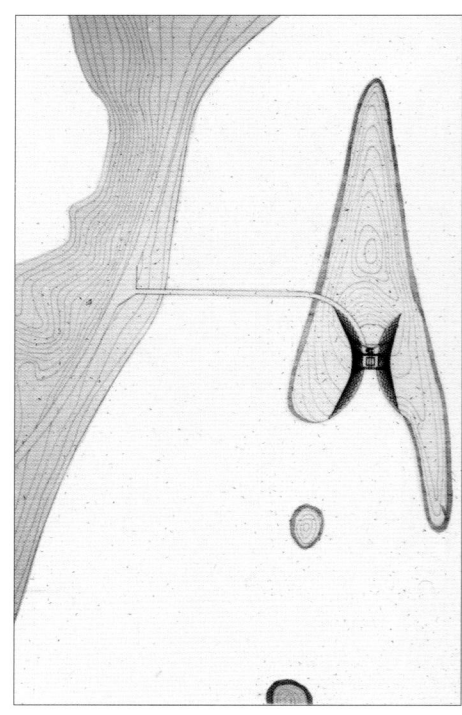

Right
Model of ABK's 1968 Canberra Bell Tower competition entry showing the bilateral lattice shells from which the high-level pod containing the bell itself is suspended.

Left
Canberra Bell Tower upper-level plan and location plan, on an island in Canberra's lake.

where the action of the sea slowly forms the gentle curve of a beach, backed by dunes or the rising land beyond. This powerful form describes the beauty of a water-to-land containment, a natural edge to seemingly limitless oceans beyond the horizon that is fundamentally different from the firm, dry land where we live – a global scene of dualities in which, comfortingly, the bay localises this universal seam between land and sea, making and marking out a special place and suggesting ideas of community.

Even at St Anne's Church, with its composite skin of light-filtering glass for both walls and roof, we find bays – one along the church walls to make a place for the choir, and the roof moulded so as to make an intermediate set of spatial particularities, like a skin that speaks of the sky, as if engaging the human spirit with a different reminiscence of containment.

I jump ahead of the bay's storyline at the Berkeley Library, a masonry building of granite, white concrete and glass with a clearly defined rectangular plan. Within, an assembly of glazed north-lit roof bays accentuate the reading room that forms the library's centre of gravity, their north light screening out the troublesome heat of the sun. In contrast, another punctuating rhythm resonates around the four walls. Bay windows of curved glass push out to frame views of Dublin's urban scene, quads, college buildings, and of people going about their business – a reminder of everyday life beyond the interior world of knowledge and ideas.

The bay recurs in later projects, on each occasion with a different function, form and material, and each lending expression to the walls and roofs.

We might consider whether, in the language of the Modern Movement, the bay or bay window can offer a meaning beyond that of the traditional classical type, stripped of inherited ornament, frills and lace. We all recognise the longstanding hierarchies of civic order established by the many representations of the temple. Many lament the loss of this tradition to what they see as the paucity of modern architecture's stripped-down materiality; the stuff that, metaphorically, you touch (or don't), along the length of precisely machine-formed glass and stainless steel facades. So perhaps in ABK's work we felt that the bay could create moments of spatial

Left
Bays from inside and out at the Berkeley Library, Trinity College Dublin. Keble College site plan in which the four-storey enclosure of the mini-quad steps down in height as the building approaches Butterfield's building at the centre of the college.

Right
A variety of bays (clockwise from top right): Inside and out at Cummins Engines; brick bays at Maidenhead Library; articulated elements for the London Docklands Light Railway; St Mary's Hospital at the Isle of Wight; Oxford Roman Catholic Chaplaincy; and Chichester College exterior and study bedroom.

extension, particularising and modelling parts of a building's edge, making elements that celebrate difference – inflections of form that offer human scale and an experience beyond the conventions of universal, thin-skinned sameness.

At Hooke Park, for John Makepeace and the Parnham Trust, we worked with the German architect/engineer Frei Otto and engineers at Buro Happold. The call for design innovation brought new structural thinking to the different building types, using uncured thinnings ('green' timber not generally in use as a building material) from the surounding forest. For the prototype student rooms and later for the adjacent workshop, different structural types, technologies and forms were developed, bending timbers in arced formations to make a new type of low-cost enclosure.

Left
Oxford Roman Catholic Chaplaincy; the White Cliffs Experience at Dover.

Right
Set in Cardiff's docks, Techniquest incorporated a new visitor centre, distinguished by a layered facade of steelwork, glazing and fabric shading, and a listed historic workshop which was renovated.

Rooflighting

In our fourth year at the Architectural Association we were set the studio task of designing a colliery workshop for a site in the Midlands. Drawn to the well-established precedent of bringing daylight into large industrial buildings by north-light roof glazing, we sought to intensify the significance of the alignments of steel roof trusses through an unconventional expression of the roof form. We developed a new awareness of how the sky and daylight contribute to our sense of orientation in interior spaces. This small beginning started us on a long path where we explored how different forms of skylight can became fundamental to the vibrancy of space and, in some cases, enhance the feel and character of a place.

Several examples come to mind. First, the glazed membrane of St Anne's Church, which provided an almost undifferentiated translucence to the cladding of the roof and walls of the church. Second, different types of roof glazing: the bay-like roof structure of the Berkeley Library, the similar forms of the Kasmin Gallery in London, and in a louvre-like stepped formation for Eastfield School hall. Likewise, the large meeting room in Oxford's Roman Catholic Chaplaincy, the roof of Portsmouth Polytechnic library, the covered walkway at Keble, the competition entry for the BT headquarters in Milton Keynes, the atriums in Dublin Dental Hospital and Offaly civic offices, and a glass roof over the generous stepped sales floors at John Lewis in Kingston upon Thames.

Third, the more restricted alignments of rooflights at Redcar Library, St Andrew's College near Dublin, the sculpture court at the Whitworth art gallery in Manchester, and in the design for the National Gallery extension, where threads of pearl-like lights would respond to the changing daylight.

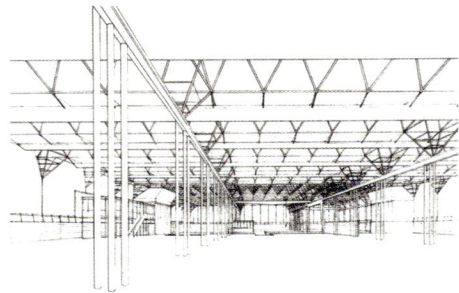

Finally, more discrete one-off rooflights that accentuate specific functions, such as the font at the Roman Catholic Chaplaincy, ward lighting at St Mary's Hospital, the cafeteria at John Lewis, the small chapel at Blanchardstown and, not least, the light above the Burton House dining table, filtered by the foliage of a plane tree.

Daylight plays a special role in ABK's work, not only in illuminating spaces deep in a building's plan,

Above
Rooflights over the reading room at the Berkeley Library, Trinity College, Dublin.

Right
Canted arrays of rooflights mark the stepped floor layers of Portsmouth Polytechnic library (1973-90).

Left
St Anne's Church in Soho, where a translucent membrane unified the roof and walls; toplit space for art at Kasmin's Gallery in New Bond Street, London (1963); rooflights provide daylight and a sense of the sky in Ahrends, Burton and Koralek's student project for a colliery workshop; rooflight at the Burton House.

but also in making a visual connection with the sky – a slice of the open universe, grey, blue, the movement of clouds and, in our temperate climate, the frequent changes of daylight caused by weather patterns. In cities we get few opportunities to appreciate the liberating grandeur of a big sky, but partial or even fragmented rooflights can offer precisely that connection.

Back on earth, wanting to punctuate and complete this review of some elements of our work, I find myself thinking of the physical realities of the construction of buildings on site. Take a winter's scene here in our northern climate: excavating earthy foundations (never to be seen again), raw north-easterly winds blowing as the concrete shuttering and reinforcing steel cages are fitted in position, truckloads of concrete lifted and placed by the latticed arms of T-shaped tower cranes (unseen men in remote high cabins) – steel, glass, pipes and then paint transforming the raw stuff to finish and complete new-made places often years after the design process was started. In parallel with this gritty and compelling pattern of physical growth I thought to remind us of this other, very different dimension to the story – that of making our designs a reality.

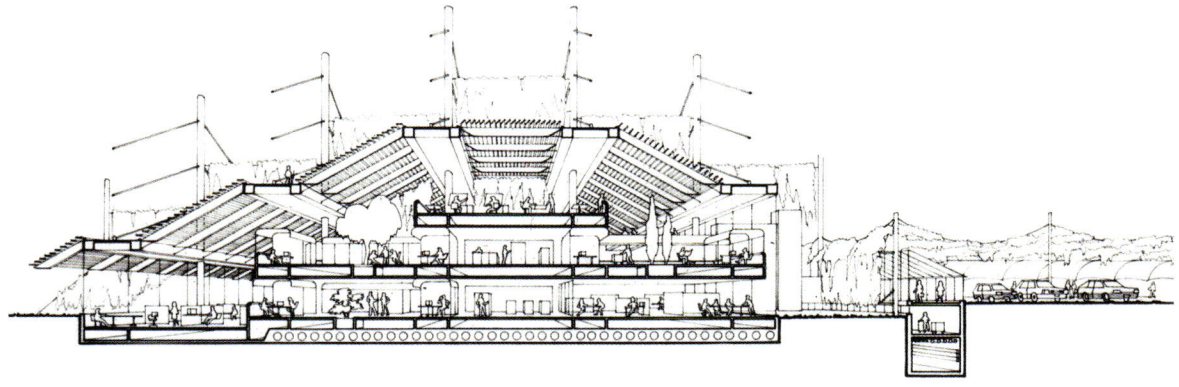

Left
Rooflights over the central circulation spaces at Dublin Dental Hospital (1991-98) and Offaly Civic Centre (1999-2002).

Right
Clockwise from top: perspective section of ABK's proposal for the British Telecom headquarters at Milton Keynes (1983); Cummins Engines factory under construction; St Andrews (1968-72); Redcar Library (1966-71), where the city council had stressed the importance of celebrating the use of structural steel, given the proximity to the Dorman Long steelworks.

A Poetic Dimension

In terms of the more poetic and abstract elements involved in the conceptual story of a design, I'd like to consider ideas that emerged in our unbuilt project for the Mary Rose Museum. Berthed in Portsmouth Harbour in 1545, Henry VIII's flagship was called into action against the French Armada which lay in wait on the Solent. Sunk with a terrible loss of life, the Mary Rose settled in the fine silt, where it remained preserved for centuries. The recovery of the surviving starboard side of the hull with its many fine artefacts was well under way when we were appointed in 1980 to design a new museum to house the vessel – a privileged opportunity that stirred our imaginations.

During the design period all that was visible was the distant silhouette of the recovery ship at anchor above the unseen hull, and a selection of beautifully preserved artefacts that had been salvaged previously from the sea bed. I hold in mind the powerful wintery image of the steely recovery ship, knowing that far below in the icy tidal currents lay the remaining timbers of the Mary Rose's hull, then offstage but soon to become a visible reminder of England's maritime history, of battles won and lost.

A cluster of dynamic cross movements grew in our minds, representations of the ship's final journey to battle, its sinking, its slow, controlled lift to the surface, and its return to a safe haven in the museum. We imagined visitors arriving along an axis that followed a curved alignment, echoing the water's edge. Then, forming a counter movement when leaving the ship hall, a raised walkway would offer visitors the option of a route extending out to sea on a small pier, returning to the comfort of a cafe on the way out. We also proposed a third alignment, placing the recovered hull on a diagonal axis, its prow pointing out to sea to the precise location of its sinking.

We intended to raise the hull high above a curved ramp so that visitors' first impression would be a sweeping view of the starboard side. In the floor below we envisaged an imprint of the hull, a memory of its 400-year resting place, while the edges of the display galleries above would echo its absent port side – a three-dimensional set of alignments that offered a spatial sense of what had been lost and was now regained.

By design, an interactive set of ideas established this conceptual and symbolic model of the museum's anatomy, with a set of forms containing the volumetric relationships of the building's parts.

At an early stage, however, we questioned the suitability of the out-of-town beachside site chosen for the museum. Predictions of visitor numbers arriving by car and coach had led Portsmouth City Council to opt for a relatively remote site to avoid congesting the city centre. Given the significance of the Mary Rose in the history of Portsmouth Naval Dockyard, it seemed a pity for the advice of traffic engineers to hold sway. Walking around the docks soon afterwards, I came across a set of seemingly underused harbour-side sheds near to the station which, if cleared, could provide a wonderful site. Making the case to our client, the Mary Rose Trust, there was some interest, but then the council members subsequently refused to reconsider the issue. We received an unambiguous instruction to design for the original site, which we did. In retrospect, it was probably overly optimistic of us to expect the council and consequently the trust to re-open a matter that had been so thoroughly assessed and agreed before we became involved.

Enter Prince Charles, who had been president of the Mary Rose Trust since its foundation in 1979. Fundraising was a key factor in the recovery of the Mary Rose, and we were asked to study how our design could be implemented in phases to first provide a modest building to accommodate the hull for a number of years while the timbers were undergoing preservative treatment. Following the presentation of our scheme we were told that the prince was looking to ABK and our consultants to waive our professional fees as a donation to the venture. After discussion, we took the view that this should be an individual decision, made freely and without any sense of royal persuasion.

We decided to decline the request, and following the raising of the hull in September 1982 were dropped without explanation as architect for the museum. Soon afterwards, it transpired that Prince Charles had accepted the idea of locating the museum in Portsmouth harbour – power begets

Above/right
Location plan for the original ABK proposal for the Mary Rose Museum; preliminary sketches by Peter Ahrends showing the development of the cranked steel roof form. The section (top) shows the remaining half of the hull with corresponding levels of visitor galleries.

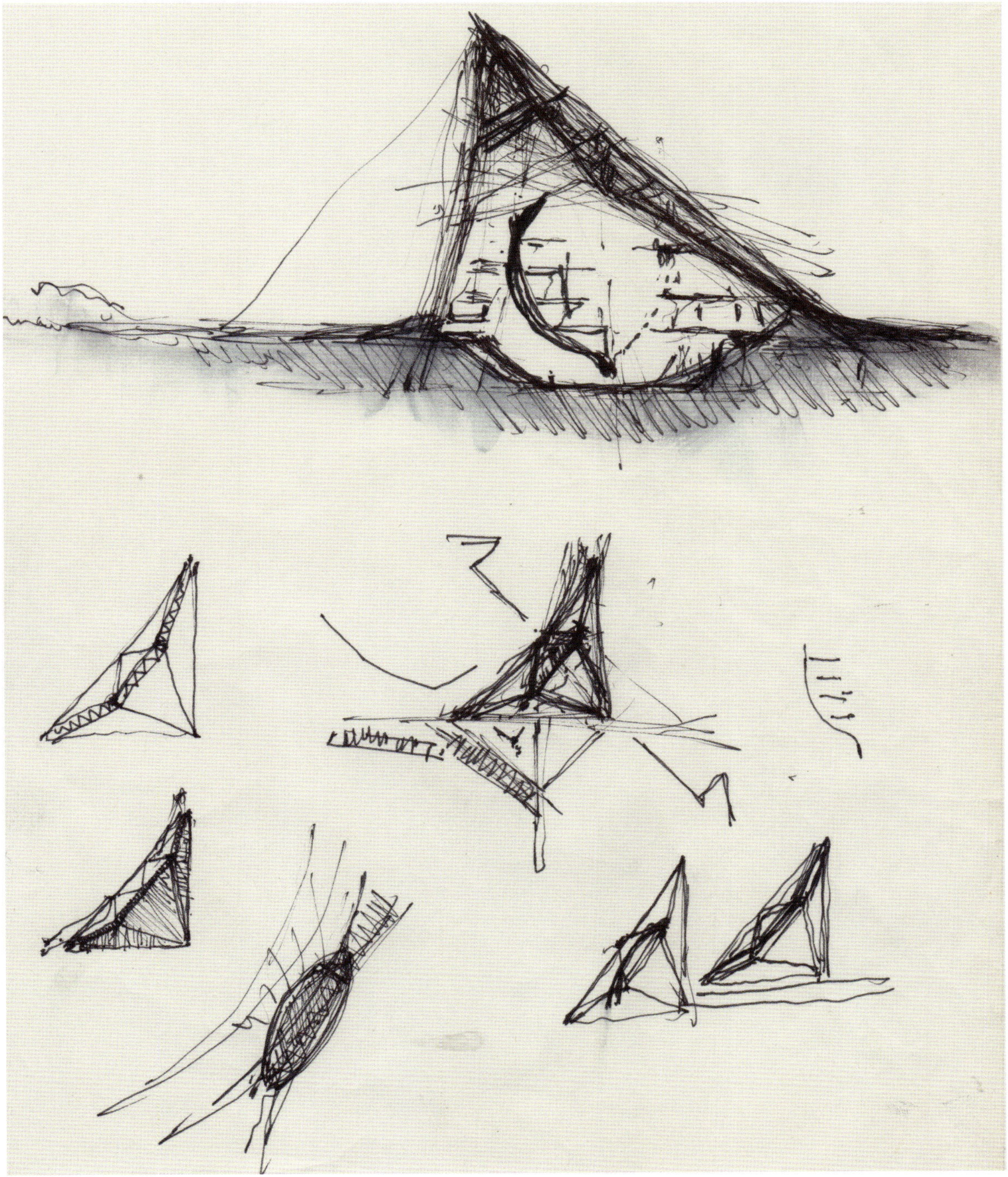

power. Whether any of this had any connection with Prince Charles' decision, years later, to damn our work for the National Gallery extension is speculation, of course.

My discussion of some of the thoughts behind our proposal for the museum is not to suggest that such ideas are formulated as separate, abstract notions. Rather that a complex process of mental oscillation draws on an intricate and interrelated range of factors, a restless search for a concept that fits, accommodates and satisfies. Nor does the user – whether city dweller, inhabitant, visitor or passer-by – need analytical prompts. Good architecture speaks for itself, without need for explanation.

Writing of modern poetry, Clive James suggests: 'The moderns not only conquered the fields of art, they conquered the fields in which art is thought about. The idea that form can be perfectly free has had so great a victory, everywhere in the English-speaking world, that the belief in its hidden technical support no longer holds up' (Poetry Notebook, 2006-14). Similarly the poetics of modern architecture?

Left
Preliminary sketches, section and model of the Mary Rose Museum illustrating routes through the building, the reconstituted floor-bed imprint and the ship's orientation to its earlier sea-bed grave; Tog Mor, the lifting vessel that raised the wreck on site in the Solent.

Right
Sketch plans for the museum by Peter Ahrends.

Bruno Ahrends: a Berlin Architect

I was born in Berlin in 1933, and my family, along with my grandparents Bruno and Hanni, remained in the city for the next few years. Disappointingly I have no memory of our times together in Berlin – nothing of Bruno's house near the Wannsee lake, nothing of the sailing, nor indeed of the general ambience. My parents emigrated to Johannesburg in 1937 when I was four, and I didn't see Bruno again as he and Hanni fled first to Italy in 1938, and were fortunate to reach England in 1939. Nor did we meet when I was in my teens as Bruno died in 1948, soon after he and Hanni had moved to live in Capetown, 800 miles distant from Johannesburg, with my émigré uncle and his young family.

During my South African childhood, the culture and character of this extended family held little meaning for me. Hardly a word was spoken about my father's family, and even less of my mother's side who lived in the south of Germany. Nor was I much aware of other far-flung family members who had fled to Australia, Ceylon, and later Bali, the USA and London – a typical diaspora in which continental separation precluded normal family connections. Was this sense of detachment disturbing, this absence with little awareness of its meanings or consequences? Surely the replacement of a familiar language and culture by another must have deeply affected my parents at the time. For me, only much later in life did I come to recognise and to some extent understand these patterns of personal loss.

In the mid-1980s I was contacted by the art historian Klaus Hinrichsen, who was helping curator Zulaika Dobson with the exhibition 'Art in Exile in Great Britain' at the Camden Arts Centre. I was able to provide some material relating to Bruno's work, and my father Steffen, by then living and working in

Andalucia, was also able to help.

Klaus had come to know Bruno in 1940-41 when they were among an extraordinary group of artists, intellectuals and lawyers who were interned at the Hutchinson Camp in Douglas on the Isle of Man. Meeting Klaus, I gave him a copies of the portrait Kurt Schwitters had painted of my grandfather, along with some of Bruno's design work of the period. The Art in Exile exhibition opened in August 1986, and Klaus gave a talk entitled 'Art in the Hutchinson Camp – a Personal View', a delightfully focussed memoir of the time when Bruno was aged 62 and Klaus just 19.

Hinrichsen takes up the story: "The well-known German architect Bruno Ahrends, who had built the Weisse Stadt Siedlung, a settlement near Berlin, within days of arrival set up a cultural department, soon popularly known as Hutchinson University. So many lecturers had staked out an area on the lawn, climbed on a chair and began to lecture in their special fields, that there were constant overlaps, worse than in Hyde Park Corner and its speakers. Nobody wanted to give way, especially not the six philosophers in the camp, who could not agree on anything, even terminology. Ahrends set up timetables for lectures and seminars and classes, especially language classes, in such a way as to eliminate clashes. He also found space for all these activities.'

'I should say an artist must do what he does best, what he is impelled to do and not be detracted into an area of ungenial work by circumstances or by sense of duty. Naturally, opinions differed, and there were some sharp exchanges. There were many different characters in the Artists Café, but the one experience all of us shared was Hitler's dictatorship, in Germany since 1933, and in Austria since the

Above
Bruno Ahrends' drawing, made in 1941 during his Isle of Man internment, is captioned 'A country house is transported from the IoM to England'. A model 'Bauhaus' villa is shown on deck, as if to suggest, despite Bruno's internment, that his Modern Movement ideals were holding true.

Opposite
Bruno Ahrends (1878-1948), painted by Kurt Schwitters in 1941 during their internment at the Hutchinson Camp. Schwitters produced more than 200 works, mostly portraits, in a 16-month period at the Hutchinson Camp. Shortage of materials led him to mix 'paint' using brick dust and oil from sardine cans, and to use lino to make prints, parcel paper, toilet paper and wallpaper, and even porridge.

Anschluss in 1937. Some of the artists, probably the majority, had left their homelands because they were Jews or of partly of Jewish descent, or had Jewish wives; others, like [Kurt] Schwitters and [Ernst] Müller-Blensdorf, had been pilloried as Degenerate Artists, or their works removed from public galleries, or in the case of Müller-Blensdorf, had seen their large war memorials destroyed in Germany and themselves blacklisted and barred from working in Germany. Many of the men had served in the first world war, Fechenbach had been badly wounded, and Bruno Ahrends had risen to the exalted military rank of Rittmeister, which I believe is equivalent to Brigadier.'

'Sixteen artists expressed their bitterness about internment in a letter which the New Statesman & Nation printed in its issue of 24th August 1940, and which read: "Art cannot exist behind barbed wire. The tension under which we live here, the sense of having suffered great injustice, the restlessness caused by proximity with thousands of other men, the worries about our wives and children...prevent us from any kind of creative activity."'

'Bruno Ahrends' utopian plans to rebuild the little town of Douglas, pulling down all existing buildings and replacing them with a few high-rise blocks and an over 20-storey hotel on the waterfront could only be imagined from being interned in Douglas: a brave new world which, luckily for the inhabitants, could not be realised!'

'And Kurt Schwitters, who was in great demand as an academic portrait painter, was the only artist who turned internment into a financial success… by no stretch of the imagination could he ever have found enough porridge… [by making his] Merz sculptures. More seriously, internment also set him on a new phase in his abstract work, although he

Right
During internment, Bruno Ahrends set himself the imaginary brief to replan Douglas with a series of tall buildings, including a harbour-front hotel.

Left
Bruno Ahrends' drawings of Hutchinson Square in Douglas, Isle of Man. The internment camp consisted of 33 houses around the square, from which tenants had been compulsorily evicted and around which a barbed wire perimeter fence erected. The Hutchinson Camp, which opened in July 1940, held up to 1,200 internees, mostly Jewish and anti-Nazi protestors from Germany and Austria.

Above
Bruno Ahrends' internment sketchbook includes many designs for Bauhaus-style buildings, including this single-storey villa.

Right
Soon after the opening of the Hutchinson Camp, the internees set up a 'university', based in the 'lecture house' on the square. Besides musical and theatrical performances, it hosted art exhibitions and lectures, including Bruno Ahrends on 'My Way to Modern Architecture'.

kept it from public view, rightly fearing disapproval and ridicule.'

And to add some of historian Monica Bohm-Duchen's closing thoughts from the Art in Exile catalogue: 'Thus, by the end of June 1940, virtually all German and Austrian nationals, about 30,000 people in all, had been interned – whether they were Jews and/or rabid anti-fascists or Nazi sympathisers. The camps set up for the purpose, most of them on the Isle of Man, were makeshift and improvised; conditions, although clearly bearing no comparison with those in camps in Germany, were hardly comfortable and communication between internees and their relatives and friends were often broken off, without warning, for weeks.'

'As it turned out, internment created conditions for greater artistic solidarity and opportunity than most of the internees had so far experienced in England. There are numerous accounts of the many artistic and intellectual activities organised on the initiative of the internees themselves (much to the bemusement, needless to say, of their guards), exploiting the ready availability of artists as well as writers, musicians and lecturers on a multitude of subjects.'

The Ahrends' family story tells that Bruno, an assimilated Jew, architect, former first-world-war cavalry officer and a keen yachtsman, had been denied membership of the exclusive Wannsee Yacht Club as a result of its anti-semitic rules. He therefore changed his name from Arons to Ahrends, re-applied and was accepted. Twenty years later, in 1942, Wannsee was to become significant as the location for the conference at which the Nazi party planned implementation of its 'Final Solution'.

There's no record of Bruno's feelings about his

Right/below
Proposal for a 'New Town' from Bruno Ahrends' internment sketchbook, dated February 1941. This intriguing scheme envisages a dense urban development two miles across with a central linear park separating residential and civic quarters, all enclosed by a ring road marked by high-rise towers.

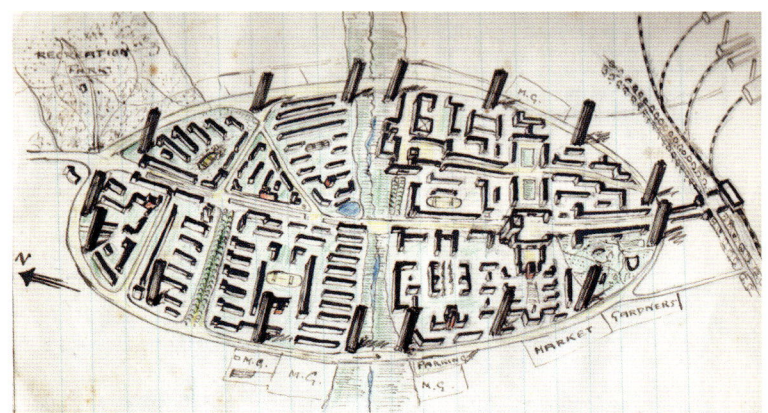

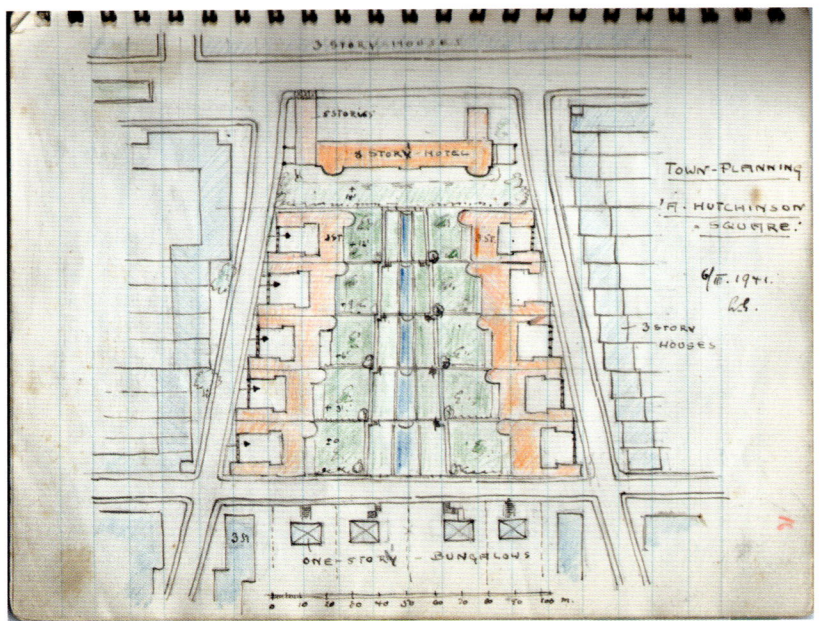

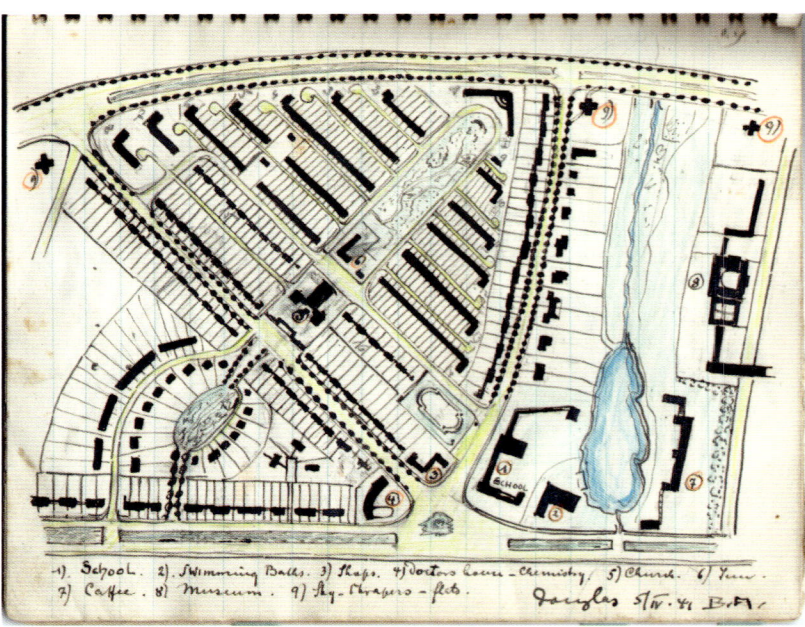

experience at the Douglas camp, but some surviving sketches suggest that his mind was actively engaged in urban matters. Years later my grandmother Hanni, who lived on in Capetown long after her husband's death, told me that when Bruno was among a group released from internment in 1941, he didn't immediately leave to return home to Cambridge. Days went by, but still no sign of her husband who, apparently, had so enjoyed the collective culture that he had helped to establish in Douglas, that he lingered for a while.

In the late-1980s, before the fall of the Berlin Wall, a history of art student in Berlin who was writing a dissertation about Bruno's work contacted me for help. Forwarding copies of the papers I had, I also referred her to Steffen and my aunt Marianne who had trained as a lawyer in pre-Nazi Berlin, left for London in the mid-1930s when she was denied the right to practice by the Nazis, and later returned to Germany in retirement.

Heimat, it seems, can override political revulsion, personal distress and anger – something that for many years was beyond my understanding. When I first returned briefly to Berlin in the late-1960s to carry out research for our practice, I felt deeply disturbed. Each day I struggled, unable to come to terms with my long-felt sense of outrage. Only by witnessing the concrete presence of the new Berlin Wall – that unambiguous symbol of separation – did I begin to comprehend the repercussions the Nazi regime had on my life.

More than 20 years later, and after the Wall came down, a reassessment of Bruno's work was under way in Berlin, so I felt that I too should start to dismantle the wall in my head by reconnecting with my long absent grandfather. I went back in the early 1990s, recognising my divided interests but

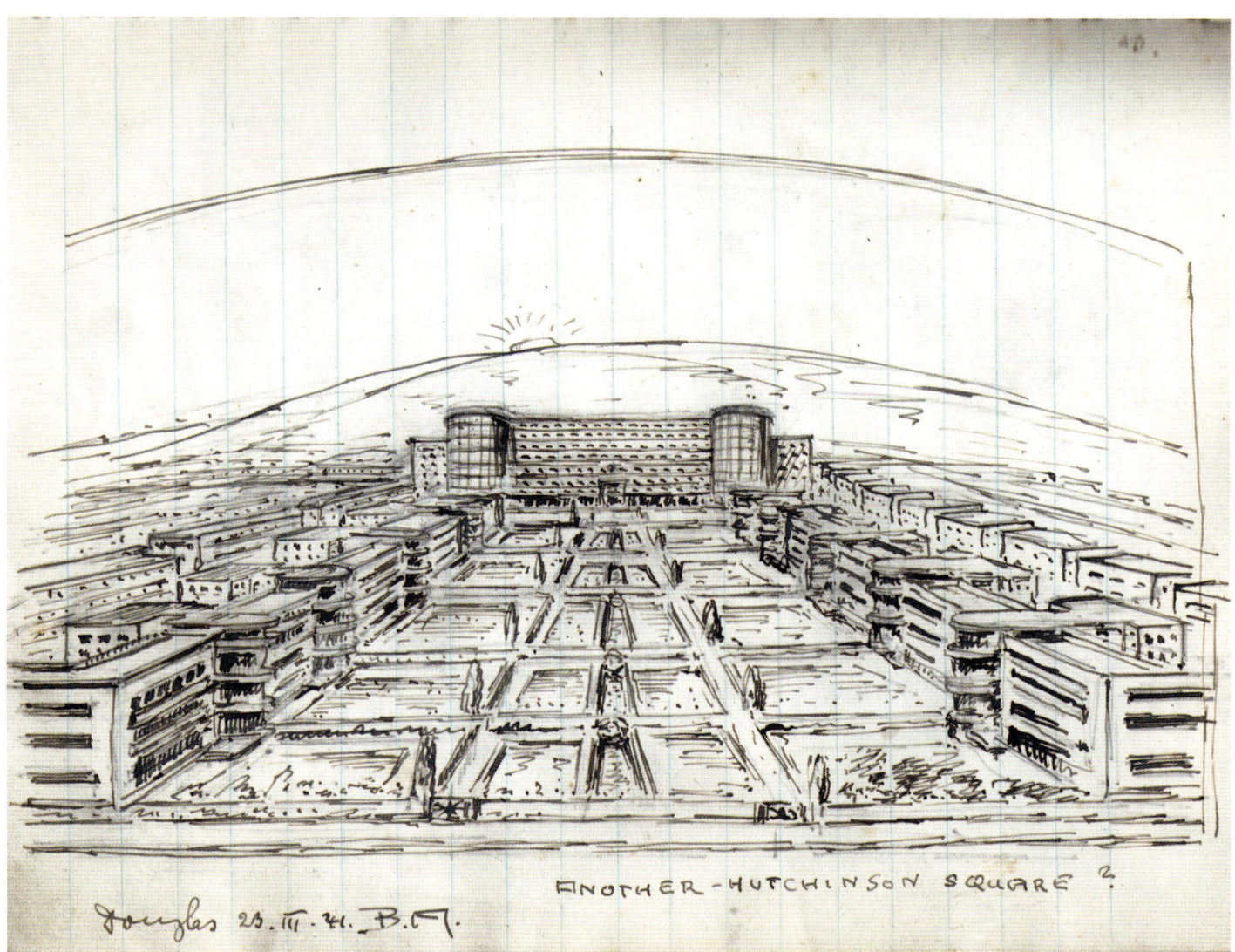

Above/left
Bruno Ahrends' ideas for replanning Hutchinson Square envisages a symmetrical arrangement centred on a hotel at its highest point and stepped terraces flanked by apartment blocks. The detailed plan (left, below), develops a sector of the New Town proposal.

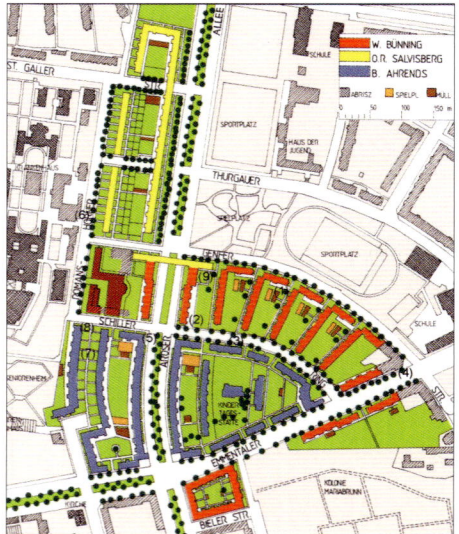

Left
The Weiße Stadt (White City) was planned in the 1920s and completed in 1931. Located in the Berlin suburb of Reinickendorf, the housing development was directed by Martin Wagner with separate districts designed by Wilhelm Büning, Bruno Ahrends and Otto Rudolf Salvisberg, who was also responsible for the masterplan. The need for low-cost, small apartments was pressing, so most comprise fewer than three rooms. Roof overhangs, rainwater pipes, doors and window frames were painted in bright colours in contrast to the white rendered walls. The development included a combined heat and power station, two laundries, a kindergarten, education and health centres, a pharmacy and 24 shops. The estate was renovated in 1949-54 following wartime damage, and updated in 1982. Bruno Ahrends was responsible for the southern sector, centred on the curved Aroserstrasse (left), which formed a gateway to the district.

accompanied by a disturbing sense of unease as I walked through the former western areas of the city on my way to an exhibition on Alexanderplatz, well before it was re-planned. On leaving I was taken by the idea of walking towards the Brandenburg Gate and following the path of the demolished Wall – symbolically a strong idea, I thought. As I walked, to my surprise, the tears began to flow, brought on by a potent mix of recalled childhood separation and the pressing reminders of presence and absence. What is an essentially space-enclosing architectural element had here served to demonstrate its divisive power – Palestine, Belfast and, in earlier times, Hadrian's Wall come to mind.

For different reasons my two subsequent visits to Berlin were also memorable. We made a tour of some of Bruno's work: white houses of the late-1920s and his most notable housing scheme, the Weisse

Stadt in Reinickendorf, one of the four social housing siedlungen, or 'settlements', planned by the office of Ahrends, Büning & Salvisberg. Each partner had been responsible for a particular sector, and Bruno's buildings – six-storey towers marking the entrance to the principle avenue – were distinguished by a quiet modern confidence. Gently curved alignments, occasional small formal inflections (reminiscent of his earlier Expressionist idiom), bay-like room extensions forming small studies, radical recognition of the significance of the kitchen within family life and, not least, a low kindergarten building situated in the safe central area of a generously proportioned garden, all contributed to a convincing model of communal living. Recognising parallels in my own interests, I was moved by the modest, unassertive strength of this urban setting. Despite the sparse number of notable architectural examplars from Britain's pre-war period, this modern resonance developed to become a potent part of the country's cultural changes during the mid- to late-twentieth century, the period in which ABK was set to work.

Bruno's architectural office grew steadily from its origins in 1920 until the 1935 Nuremberg Laws forbade him to practice beyond 1937. There's no reference to a precise closure date in his letters from this time, but Steffen, who worked in his father's office for a number of years after his return from Ernst May's group in Moscow, later wrote that it had become clear that further work in a modern idiom would be forbidden, and 'only steep pitched roofs' – identifiably part of the national German vernacular – would be acceptable.

Bruno was forced to retire at 59, an age when many architects are reaching their professional peak. I understand he arranged for one of his trusted (and

Above/left
Bruno Ahrends' practice thrived during the inter-war period, producing a series of villas in Berlin, including Kyllmannstrasse (above) and (left) Wachtelstrasse.

presumably non-Jewish) senior assistants to run the studio, with him acting as informal consultant, until the ongoing work was completed. Steffen left for Johannesburg at the beginning of 1937. Bruno's other sons and his daughter were by then emigrés living in Australia, South Africa and England. He himself travelled to Rome in 1938, living alone for much of the time in a modest pensione in what he described as 'the heart of the city'.

It is difficult to understand why Bruno, having left Germany five years after Adolf Hitler became chancellor, chose to move to Italy, just three years after Mussolini had been legally installed as dictator. Why not choose London, for instance, where his daughter Marianne had settled. Maybe he thought an eventual return to Germany would be feasible. Or perhaps he was attracted by the cultural weight of Italy, a country he had visited previously with his parents. Or maybe he had noted the Fascist regime's promotion of modern architecture, witnessed in the work of Giuseppe Terragni, Adalberto Libera and others, that contrasted with the Nazi party's predilection for neoclassicism and the vernacular Heimatstil. He also may have assumed that, as a former officer in the German army during the first world war, he would be less than welcome in Britain.

Bruno remained in Rome until April 1939, passing the time by assiduously drawing the city's historic buildings. He did however, express some enthusiasm for the Italian 'new towns', visiting Sabaudia which had been built five years earlier on the Pontine marshes south of Rome, and wrote about applying his reparation planning ideas in the aftermath of the Spanish Civil War. Given the extent to which social housing was central to Bruno's Berlin work, it's difficult to make anything of these apparent contradictions. Perhaps he didn't see them

Above/right
Bruno Ahrends' water-colour drawings, made on board the HMS Ormonde, while en route to England in March 1938.

Left
Escaping Berlin for Rome, Bruno Ahrends spent much of his time drawing street scenes, monuments and architectural detail.

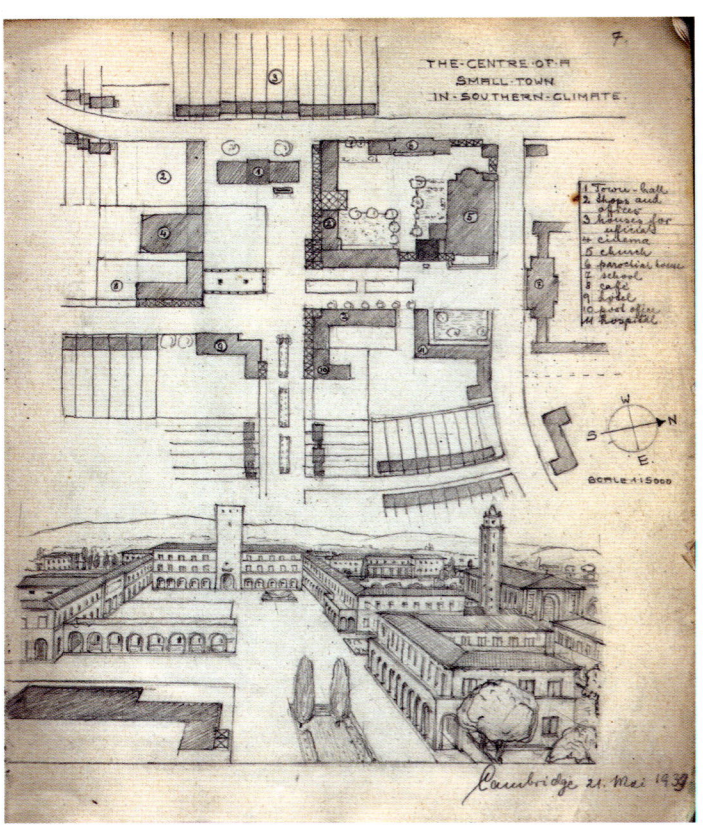

as contradictions, but with his working life curtailed, sought to look beyond the repressive political situation to formulate ideas for a different future.

Architecture carries powerful social and political values, and these are especially evident in Bruno's housing projects. In any case, are there not also contradictions in my own work? Given my views about Palestine and Israel's occupation of the West Bank, why did ABK work in the Jewish quarter of Jerusalem's old city in the late 1960s? To the extent that I gave any clear thought to political issues at the time, I was naive and optimistic that democracy could prevail in what later became a repressively divided state. But the question stands, if only to remind us that each commission brings with it political values, however embedded and implicitly 'normal' these may seem at the time.

Bruno joined Hanni in London in April 1939 – the story goes that he had received a cable from Berlin saying: 'don't come back', although there's no document to confirm this. However, Bruno's annotations to his sequence of watercolour sketches reveal the dates of his travels as:

Roma 24/5/1938 to 25/02/1939
Sorrento 27/02/1939
Capri 28/02/1939
Napoli 01/03/1939
Minorca 04/03/1939 (from the MS Ormande)
English Channel 08/03/1939 (ditto)
Cambridge 08/04/1939
Douglas, Isle Of Man 28/01/1941 to 25/02/1942
Cambridge and Oxford 1939-43
Hout Bay, Capetown 25/05/1948

After the war Bruno and Hanni left Britain to make their lives in South Africa, but within months of their arrival in Capetown in 1948 Bruno died, aged 70. In the few sketches made in South Africa,

Above/right
Views of Cambridge, 1940.

Left
Proposal for 'The Centre of a Small Town in Southern Climate', dated 1939, soon after Ahrends had arrived in Cambridge. The picturesque arrangement draws both on Cambridge quads and Ahrends' recent stay in Rome, where he visited Mussolini's 'new town' of Sabaudia.

Proposed garden court of a bungalow at Colombo, between dining-room and kitchen-wing.   C. 22/11.39.

the sensitivity evident in his earlier drawings was, not surprisingly, no longer there.

During the war, in the period of his stay in Oxford and Cambridge, Bruno was asked to give a lecture on 'Modern Architecture and the Modern Architect'. The talk closed with an enthusiastic reference to two schools then under construction near Cambridge. Given the ambition of his ideas for the modern reconstruction of the centre of Douglas, prepared during his internment, in delivering this lecture he surely would have felt the pain of thwarted aspiration: a modern architect of Berlin working during the Bauhaus period, unable to stay on in Berlin. My grandparents escaped fate in the gas chambers and found a safe refuge in England. Hanni worked as a housekeeper to make ends meet, but Bruno never worked again.

Right
Hanni with punts in 1943, and with Bruno at home in Cambridge.

Left
Watercolour sketch of Arthur Blomfield's St Barnabas, Oxford.

Opposite
Courtyard of a proposed villa in Columbo, dated 1939. By this date Bruno's extended family, fleeing Nazi Germany, had scattered as far as Ceylon.

Steffen Ahrends: Berlin, Moscow, Johannesburg and Andalucia

I hesitate in telling Steffen's story, not quite knowing where to start. I loved my father but despite our closeness in other respects, we never found it easy to talk in depth about architecture. Had it been otherwise, we might have been able to share more of the significant events in our lives, what we believed in. Perhaps this was not surprising. By my late teens I had decided to study architecture – a world to which, I guess, Steffen would have so wanted to welcome me. In supporting my plan to move to London, he'd have known that I might come to make a new life thousands of miles from Johannesburg, a place that he would not have chosen for himself, had he been free to do so as a young architect in the late 1930s. For my part, aged 18 and determined to go, I didn't appreciate then that this could mean leaving behind South Africa, a country that I later came to realise had never really felt like home.

Finding a way into Steffen's life as an architect, I recognise that it was to England too that his own parents had fled. Mine was no such flight, so I thought he'd understand. Just as the politics of Nazism had disrupted and then prevented the working relationship with his father Bruno, a generation later, with the Nationalists' policy of apartheid taking hold, my departure would cause him further loss. This moving reading evokes my childhood memories of that single fracture in the seemingly solid substance of a stone boulder.

Steffen arrived in Johannesburg early in 1937 at the age of 30. He found work and a place to live, and my mother and I joined him several months later. Some 25 years later, running a successful practice, he wrote a thesis in support of his associate application to the Royal Institute of

British Architects, which included a summary of Johannesburg's colonial architectural history as a background to his own work. He refers to the closing days of the city's 1936 Empire Exhibition (celebrating the 50th anniversary of the Witwatersrand Gold Rush that resulted in its founding), which leads me to imagine how the culture shift represented by his new life – symbolised perhaps by the pale yellow sand of the goldmine 'dumps' – gave rise to a haze whose causes lay rather deeper than the natural phenomena of the strong dust-laden winds. For all its merits, Johannesburg was neither Berlin nor Moscow, global cities where he'd worked as a young architect with such hope and aspiration.

Nor was it London, where I would arrive 14 years later during the closing weeks of the Labour government's great Festival of Britain. Even if I had been aware of these family histories at the age of 18, would I have been struck by such remote similarities? Consider too the parallels between Bruno's Italian 'study period' in Italy of 1938-39 and mine in Tuscany during the summer of 1951 when, though under very different political circumstances, we were both en route to England.

When I left South Africa to study in London I held few considered views of Steffen's architectural work, which mostly comprised large (yet seldom materially lavish) houses for the wealthy white ruling class. When I returned to work in his office for a spell, l was a different person. Five years at the AA had begun to shape my beliefs, aspirations and political views as well as my confidence to formulate criticism and engage in discussion.

Steffen had a remarkable ability to connect with his clients, recognising their needs and designing fitting yet unheroic houses using local materials that offered them new ways to live their lives. His architectural vocabulary of restrained plasticity played down the evident 'ease' of class-ridden wealth, offering a comfortable and 'ordinary' openness to climate and context that served to make these houses individual – he made his clients feel special.

Cultured yet unpretentious, he grew up during the Weimar Republic and was educated in the Bauhaus spirit at Weimar. On graduating, he had accepted an invitation from Ernst May to join his group of dedicated young architects working in Moscow in the early-1930s. Years later, in practice in South Africa, Steffen clearly recognised the significance of the racist divisions of the late-colonial politic long before the National Party's apartheid policies had hardened and set in.

It is difficult to reconcile the contradictions in Steffen's consciousness of the growing oppression of the black majority while working with success and artistry for the wealthy, white ruling class. On the one hand, the constraints of the prevailing political establishment, and on the other, the need to make a life and a living in architecture. And this in a place in which he had not freely chosen to settle; nor was it an outcome that could have been predicted during his life in Berlin in the late-1930s.

Steffen takes up the story: 'Having in front of my eyes the Cape Peninsular, one of the world's most beautiful districts, I arrived in Johannesburg, seeing the city in the late afternoon sun behind yellow mine dumps – truly deserving the name Golden City'.

This large city, spreading over nearly 80 square miles with a population of about 700,000, black and white, was just 50 years old, and Steffen's initial impressions of the inequalities were apparent.

Left
Born in Berlin, Steffen Ahrends (1907-92) attended the Weimar Bauhochschule, studying under Otto Bartning and Ernst Neufert. He joined Ernst May's Group in Moscow in 1931 but returned to his father's studio in 1932. In 1937 he emigrated to South Africa, where he built up a successful practice. He left in 1972 to live in Spain.

Above
Steffen with his mother Hanni in Johannesburg in the late 1950s.

'Here, Non-White people have always lived separately from the Whites in compounds, slummy locations or shanty towns, with a home life of complete "apartheid" long before that word was coined, and the government created huge townships of monotonous row-upon-row of soul-destroying square boxes… in comparison, even the poorest white person lives in luxurious surroundings.'

'With the exception of only one house that I was honoured to design and build for an African, a relatively privileged doctor, all the houses were for Europeans (and their numerous Non-White servants)… I have worked as an architect in Johannesburg for 25 years, having built more than 200 houses. What has made these houses something special may be difficult to explain. Their variations are manifold and they are neither a "type" nor of one particular vernacular, but it appears that they have now become an integral portion of this amazing city.'

'Of particular interest are the forces and ideas which may change the pattern of living in Johannesburg, which has not been subjected to any great changes since the city was founded 70 years ago. This symbolises the coming end of an era which in other parts of the world would have already become an anachronism.'

Right
Steffen Ahrends' Transvaal Chamber of Mines Pavilion, built for the 1953 Rand Show in Johannesburg.

Above/right
Steffen Ahrends' practice thrived in Johannesburg, where he designed around 500 houses. Stylistically varied, they tended to employ traditional local materials and construction methods.

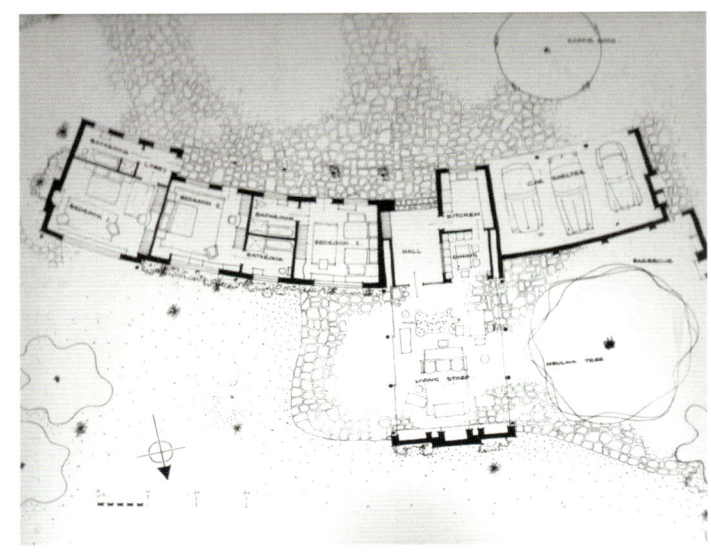

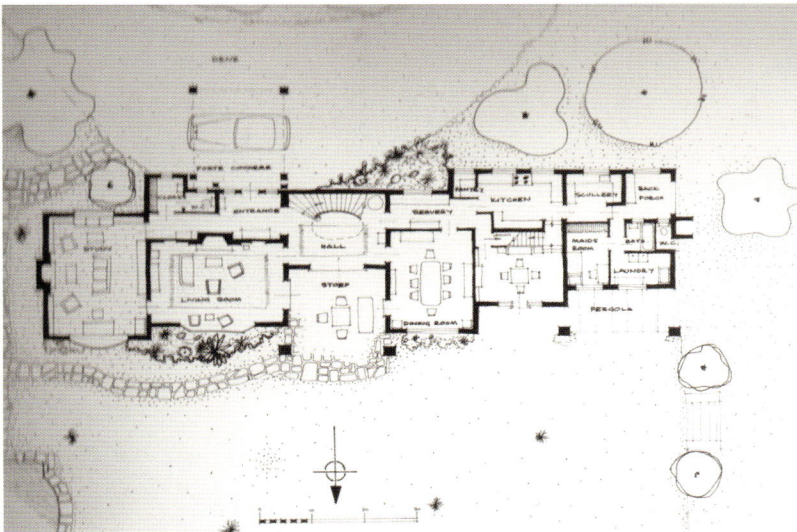

'Finally, one positive thought to counterbalance the effect of these expected changes: an integrated multi-racial social system may eliminate the fear complex and enable all people in this town to have a more positive approach towards the future. The traditional (White) house will then lose its validity and die a natural death. The past will be past and the contemporary house will become an integral part of tomorrow's living.' Writing this more than a dozen years after the Nationalist government's enactment of its apartheid policies, it is clear that Steffen was never reconciled to long-term racist divisions.

Looking back to his early years, Steffen writes: 'I was born in Berlin in 1907 during a period of Wilhelminic splendour and the culmination of German Imperialist power at the time when the first rumblings of Socialism were heard in Europe.'

'My father was an architect', he writes, 'and his professional education had been conventional so that he was well-versed in period styles, but he was already inclined not so much towards Art Nouveau but rather in the direction of a new movement that Adolf Loos in Austria and Hermann Muthesius in Germany had brought to light. He had quit the government service and worked as a junior partner with one of Berlin's well-known architects until the outbreak of war in 1914.'

'Our background was typical of the wealthy upper-middle class. One grandfather was an autocratic Wilhelminic ruler of a large publishing house, the other was a banker, who spent his ample leisure time travelling the world, playing music and collecting objects d'art. The Wilhelminic era was finished but the revolution was throttled; the staying power of the bourgeoisie had been too great.'

Above/right
Steffen Ahrends built a bungalow for his family on a sloping, rocky site, in which the cranked plan follows the contours.

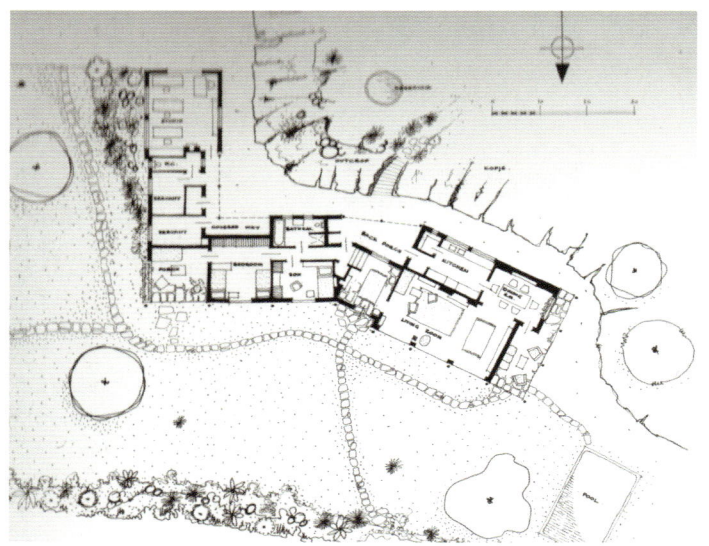

'As an example of the post-war approach to life, coupled with an insight that young architects should learn, I thought to experience how tradesmen use their tools, how materials should be handled and how to coordinate the hundreds of small details that result in a well-finished building, I worked during my holidays, and afterwards for more than a year, with carpenters, bricklayers and joinery men on various buildings in Berlin. Beside the practical understanding and technical knowledge gained it resulted in a far deeper experience and… contact with the working class, their problems and thoughts, their trade unionism, never-ending discussions on Socialism and criticism of mismanagement… an awakening from the dreams of a protected childhood into the realities of a new kind of life in which it was believed that the solution of Europe's problems would come from the East.'

'The Bauhaus period in Weimar moved to new buildings in Dessau. In the same year Professor Bartning, well-known for his church in Cologne, assembled some of the best pupils and assistants the Bauhaus had produced and restarted a new school of architecture in the vacated Bauhaus building.'

'This "second edition" of the Bauhaus, based on the Dessau concept, had the same type of workshops for industrial design and the same positive approach to what was then called the International Style. In those days we (students and masters), believed ourselves to be the pillars of a new world. When in 1927 we saw Le Corbusier's two houses at the Weissenhof exhibition in Stuttgart (planned by Mies van der Rohe) we admired his genius for a period of two weeks then tore his work to pieces. Frank Lloyd Wright, although highly respected as a "grand old master", was à priori considered passé. Mies van der Rohe, whose Barcelona Pavilion and beautiful house in the Berlin Exhibition had not yet been built, was greatly admired for his precision of thought; but we then believed that he would end in a cul-de-sac. Only Gropius, who never came back to Weimar, was considered beyond criticism. For us the history of architecture started with the Soviet 1917 revolution.'

'The years between 1929 and 1939 were decisive in my life, with one year in my father's firm in Berlin when he gave me a free hand in designing various types of modern farmhouses for the 1930 Berlin Building Exhibition. These were interesting insofar as some units were prefabricated, being erected in less than a day, while others used new and untried building materials. Now they appear box-like and crude double-storeyed monstrosities, forced "modern" and unimaginative.'

'Although during the years 1918 to 1933 Berlin was considered the intellectual and artistic centre of Europe, other influences were stronger. With great excitement I accepted an offer in 1931 to work with the group formed by Ernst May (the city architect in Frankfurt, well-known for his modern schools and large housing schemes), who had gone to Moscow for the planning of new Socialist towns of the first Five Year Plan.'

'In those years, for most young men living in the centre of western Europe, Russia was more than "the Socialist Sixth of the World". Only a dozen years had passed since the revolution and we saw in her what we wanted to see – not so much the Socialist system – but the beginning of a new and better world, a new code that had broken with the rigid conventions of the bourgeois era. The new Russian theatre, the first famous films and novels, the "functionalist" architecture gripped us and, in our imaginations, it was obvious that the solution

Left
Working in the office of his father Bruno Ahrends in 1930, Steffen was responsible for the design of a series of buildings for the Berlin Building Exhibition.

Right
In 1929 Frankfurt city architect Ernst May was invited to Moscow to collaborate on the USSR's first Five Year Plan, which aimed to build mass-produced workers' flats to house two million additional people within Moscow's urban core. Steffen Ahrends joined the group in 1931.

to our dreams and expectations was close at hand.'

'Those two years in Moscow did more to us than just dampen our enthusiasm, they opened our eyes and we learned to differentiate between the good and the bad. The purges and subsequent revelations of completely totalitarian rule started after 1933. We went to Russia to see whether this "newest world" might not become our future home. The Russian architects had been fantastic designers, dreaming up schemes of limitless possibilities, experimenting architecturally in all directions.'

'In our group of thirty architects, typical German efficiency ruled; town planning, systematic developments of standard houses and flats, schools, hospitals, recreation and shopping centres – all "rubber stamped" and neatly worked out to the last standard detail. Very little was built, as guns had priority over butter.'

'Convinced that a totalitarian state was not one that I would voluntarily choose to live in, I returned to Germany just in time to witness Hitler's final rise to power and, thereafter, not only the complete collapse of liberalism and everything that had made German culture so valuable in the 14 years of democracy, but the rise of a totalitarian state; far worse than anything anticipated. Work of the Modern Movement (including architecture) was destroyed. Neoclassicism and the desire for false monumentality coupled with a revival of a sentimental "home" style (the peasant and his importance), were instated for political purposes.'

'This started an exodus of a great number of intellectuals who were not prepared to breathe air so dangerously threatening. Anybody who could or had to leave started looking for a place where he could live in relative freedom.'

He concludes: 'In 1935 my membership of the Institute of Architects was cancelled – under their ingenious new classification I suddenly "became" non-Ayran. I helped my father in his practice until the end of 1936 and then decided to leave for South Africa'.

So, it would seem that it was touch-and-go whether I would be born in Moscow or Berlin. But Berlin it was to be. With my mother's pregnancy in the late summer of 1932 and with the Nazi party not yet in power, I guess you take the obvious step of going home to make a life, don't you? Just then, their return to Berlin's culture must have seemed like an exciting, hopeful plan, but this was to be increasingly undermined by my parents' growing anxieties in the four years that followed.

If I understand it correctly, it was my non-Jewish mother, Visino, no longer working as a Bauhaus-period weaving instructor, who had a clearer view of the growing anti-semitism on the streets of Berlin. Time to leave, to emigrate to South Africa; a different world with the challenge of a new

Above/right
The Social Science and Speech Clinic at the East Campus of the University of the Witwatersrand in Johannesburg, built in 1963 by Steffen Ahrends & Partners.

language and probably little by way of culture. And, at the time, without knowing that racism was soon to emerge there too.

In the early 1970s, visiting Andalucia to design houses near the golf courses for his South African clients, Steffen was approached by a much younger architect, Aubrey David, to form a new partnership. Here they would design holiday homes for the Costa de Sol's fast-developing tourist industry.

By now in his early 60s, Steffen decided to move to the Spanish coast, soon to design and settle in Bahia-de-Casares, a remote, newly-built settlement on the Andalucian coastline near the beautiful mountainside settlement of Casares.

With the military dictatorship of General Franco still holding power in Spain, the move from South Africa may seem rather ironic, but for a young family this open, sunny place on the southern edge of Europe would offer a hopeful way out of the repressive politics of apartheid, another new beginning.

In terms of Steffen's work and family life it proved a good move. His energy renewed, he took to every new opportunity with gusto, and produced good work with his young partner. He found new formal expressions in his designs and, not least, built a hill-top house for his family with views across the Mediterranean towards Morocco's Atlas Mountains, a reminder, perhaps, of the vast African continent he had left behind.

In due course, however, Spain's economic bubble burst and the development market dried up. Without work Steffen returned to South Africa, taking up his retained position in the practice. It was not a good time. Ill-at-ease and perturbed by the entrenched political scene, he longed to return

to Spain. Eventually he did, but for Steffen this move marked the end of his career.

To his disappointment Steffen had been unable to find architectural work back in Spain. In the aftermath of recession little was being built in this tourist-dependent region. Bare concrete frames of broken Mediterranean investments stood as stark reminders of the recurrent patterns of boom and bust, skeletons punctuating the otherwise beautiful coastline. Although Steffen never quite came to terms with retirement from practice, he found creative satisfaction in pottery and painting during his later years.

Just as political events and the consequential economic crises had shaped the latter stages of Bruno's professional life, so, less traumatically, did they affect the Steffen's later years. Such patterns of disruption and incompletion are not uncommon – the career of architect Charles Rennie Mackintosh comes to mind, as do those of the painter Kurt Schwitters and author James Joyce – but architecture has little shared social meaning when it remains unbuilt, without material substance and above all, uninhabitable.

As the art of place-making, architecture offers aesthetic dimensions as it rubs shoulders with time, changing the hard-edged qualities of urban contexts. To be denied a fulfilling role in this complex process by the traumatic repercussions of anti-semitism must have been tough. For Bruno in Rome, this loss was surely not satisfied by a pen and sketchbook. And I don't ignore my feelings of sadness for how Bruno and Steffen must have felt. Yet both had full lives that now occupy a vivid place in my mind.

Left/right
After moving to Spain's Costa del Sol in 1972, Steffen Ahrends worked with Aubrey David on the design of a cluster settlement of villas on a hill near Estepona, a showpiece development that has subsequently been given protected status.

An Early Childhood in Berlin

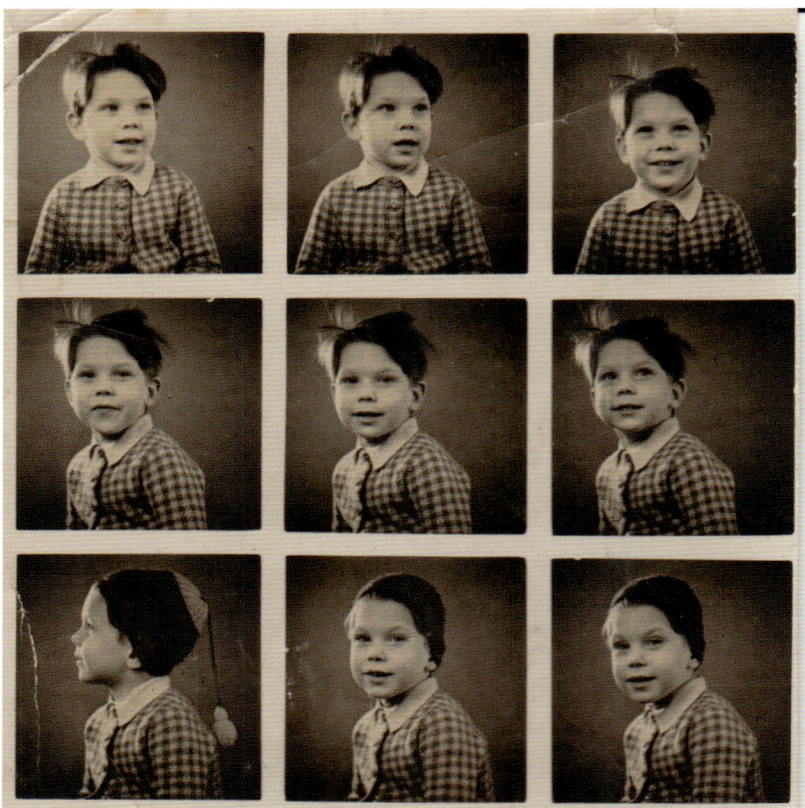

During a very hot June in 1987 Richard Burton and I made our first working visit to Moscow at the onset of what became the long haul of ABK's project for the new British Embassy. There we were both touched by aspects of our family histories: Richard trying to find clues in search of his pre-revolutionary ancestral home, and me vaguely picking at a few threads of my feelings about my parents' stay in Moscow in the early 1930s; their hopes in contributing to the construction of new urban settlements in the Soviet Union and, not least, my conception in the summer of 1932.

This is not to suggest that the culture of Stalin's communism had some kind of prenatal effect on my life but rather to recognise this now elusive layer of my parents' early history; their stay in Moscow as but a small part of an appreciation of the history and action of revolutionary change, and my affirming view of a creative wave of design energy, extending from Cubism, Russian Constructivism, the radical influence of the Bauhaus, and the reactionary reversal of Russia's Socialist Realism and the disasters of Nazi oppression.

Did this exert some kind of influence on my early childhood? In Berlin we lived in an apartment in Bruno Taut's newly-completed Onkel-Tom's-Hütte, a utopian housing project in Zehlendorf and one of the city's four Weimar Republic siedlungen.

But formative? Perhaps it was a good start, and one that may say something about the aspirations of my parents; the dream of building a new world which, though soon to be threatened by the second world war, lived on in Attlee's British government in the late-1940s, Castro's Cuba, or Allende's Chile. I appreciate such examples are few, and that global capitalism is evidently and powerfully pervasive,

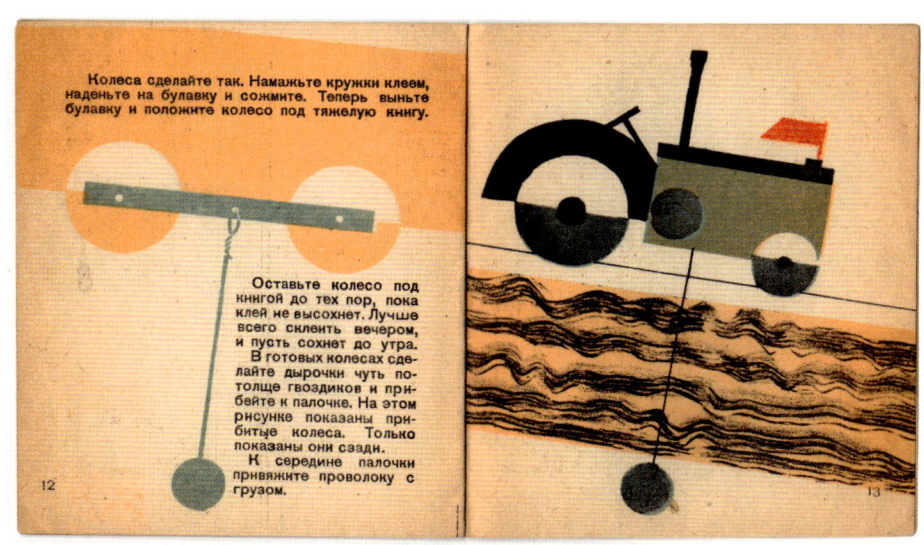

Above
While working in Moscow in 1931, Steffen Ahrends and his wife bought childrens' booklets for their future son, Peter.

Right
Sketch by Richard Burton of St Basil's Cathedral in Moscow.

Opposite
A youthful Peter Ahrends poses in a photo-booth.

Left
1933 album with Peter and his father Steffen. The family's Berlin home was in Bruno Taut's Onkel-Tom's-Hütte housing development.

Opposite
A page from the Soviet-era childrens' booklets that Steffen bought for Peter from Moscow; aerial view of Southampton Docks in their heyday.

despite the economic disasters of its inherent fault-lines. But not to be unchangeable, forever?

Returning to the mid-1930s, I possess a collage of memories. A set of open-sided Bauhaus-type play cubes, plywood, coloured, probably made by my father, and big enough for a two- or three-year-old to squeeze into, store things in or just scatter around the room. In London, 25 years later, I would make some child-habitable hinged plywood play structures for our young daughters, Jacqui and Jane, scarcely recognising then this family 'tradition'.

At around this time, Steffen rowed out to the middle of the Wannsee. He had returned from Moscow with (to eager Nazi eyes) 'dangerous' Communist literature, which now he hoped to lose in the lake, only to find that paper floats. Thankfully excluded from the cull were a number of fold-out children's books with characteristic Constructivist graphics that my parents had bought for me. Later, pinned to my nursery walls in Johannesburg, they formed pictorial stories for many a year, and they remain largely intact on my shelves to this day.

These thoughts trigger a teenage memory of a story told to me by a politically active Berlin émigré, then living in South Africa. When in Berlin, he and his friends had devised an ingenious means to distribute anti-Nazi pamphlets in quantity and without being seen. They suspended a string cradle loaded with the pamphlets from the nozzle of a watering can, and placed the contraption on a roof parapet high above a busy street. Having made several small holes in the bottom of the can, ensuring that it could safely tip forward without falling, they filled it with water and quickly left the building. Slowly, the water leaked out until the can, loaded with its precious political bundles, tipped forward, raining the pamphlets down upon the street below. The story rhymes loosely with my fascination for flowing water, whether in streams, with their many associations and meanings, or in powerful rivers like the Thames whose place-making meanings lie deep in our urbanising 'genes'.

The old family friend, probably not Jewish, who had given my parents money to flee Nazi Germany had advised them to first have me baptised, suggesting they might find it helpful in South Africa. It was done, despite my parents' lack of any religious conviction, in a Catholic church. Marked for life? Does the memory of that uncomfortable dab of cold water on my forehead still do battle with my atheism? Such recollections evoke times of political movement and radical change, though it's hard to judge their effect, if any, on a three-year-old.

Two further memories, both also associated with water and movement, bring a different flavour. The first is from Berlin in the winter of 1936-37, just after my father had left for Johannesburg. My uncle Bobby is skating backwards on a large frozen pond, holding my hands to pull me through the bustling crowd, and I'm feeling exhilarated by this magical new experience. Was it the feel of the ice or the busy movement of the crowd that seemed so special?

Fast-forward some months, and my mother and I are arriving in Southampton to board a liner bound for South Africa. The overwhelming presence of the huge hull grabbed me, just like Richard Serra's steel sculptures have since – a resonance without clear meaning, but associated with a sense that we were on the move, destination unknown to me.

Analogous in some respects to the early stages of the process of designing buildings? Ideas emerging without certainty, the pen encouraging the flow of mark-making on paper; condensed black-ink descriptions of imagined forms, spaces, places.

A Grounded Afterword

A selection of anecdotal sketches illustrating other significant and memorable moments.

1935/38/41 Upside Down

This is neither a reference to my family's 1937 other-way-up journey from Berlin to the southern hemisphere, nor to artist Joaquín Torres García's 1936 drawing depicting an inverted map of South America, but rather to a number of near drownings that occurred in my early childhood.

Aged three, tipping forward, head and shoulders first, into the watery depths of a rainwater barrel in my grandparents' Berlin garden. Fear doesn't figure in the memory – just the struggle to get my body the right way up.

Then at the age of five and not yet a swimmer, I fell again while reaching out to save a struggling insect near the edge of a Johannesburg garden swimming pool. There seemed to be no one around as I bobbed up and down, but soon my mother, wondering where I was, came to the rescue.

Third time, I was clambering around with a friend in a gentle rock-strewn stream that, following an up-river summer storm, suddenly became a full flowing brown-water torrent. Both clinging for our lives to boulders, we were eventually rescued by a farmer from the opposite bank.

The power of these watery moments left me with lasting impressions. Elsewhere I have mentioned the affinity I feel for the flow of water (streams, rivers, ocean tides, breakers in coastal bays), which for me seems to have had an ever-present but unconscious presence in the process of design. Little wonder.

1953 A Revolution and Deflation

K,B and A made a summer trip to Greece, travelling overland in a second-hand London taxi, a sturdy mid-1940s vintage with a black leather fold-down roof over the passenger compartment.

We drove in shifts through the night. At dawn I find myself at the wheel on a new, straight-line highway between Belgrade and Zagreb in President Tito's communist Yugoslavia. Paul is beside me on our DIY 'passenger' seat (where, in times of old, luggage was placed), and Richard is sound asleep in the back. My eyes close for a second, opening just as we start to veer towards the embankment. My reactive tug on the wheel coupled with sharp braking causes the taxi to spin. Completing a full revolution, we end up facing the right way but on the wrong side of the road. There's no other traffic on the road and as Paul and I inspect the vehicle for damage, Richard begins to stir, sleepily asking: 'Where are we?'. Back in the driving seat and setting off again I find myself thinking that revolution can be OK and that breakfast would be good.

Travelling in our much-admired taxi from Mount Athos down to Delphi, I find myself feeling vaguely uncomfortable with the grand symbols of the past. This wasn't so much to do with the aesthetic dimensions of the architecture but rather with the distorted ethos of monastic authority and the assertive impositions of classical temples.

As our thoughts turn to homebound travel, we ask ourselves whether we can afford a Piraeus to Brindisi ferry-crossing rather than the long haul back overland? Yes, but at the dockside on the morning of departure, tickets in hand, we find that the taxi, with its fixed roof rack, is too high to pass through the ship's loading dock. We release the tyre pressures all round to find that, here at least, deflation works well.

Above
Simonas Petras Monastery, Mount Athos, Greece. Built on a single rock some 330 metres above the sea, the building dates back to the thirteenth century.

1955　Papa Longues Jambes and Paul's Wound

Early in the autumn term's run-up to our final-year stint at the AA, five of us take the newly-available Volkswagen 'bus' on a pilgrimage across central France to see Corb's recently completed church at Ronchamp. It's early evening as I struggle to drive safely through the French fog when our guardian angel kicks in to take control, steering us away from the underside of a huge oncoming camion with inches to spare (these were pre-metric times). Lights flashing, horn screaming, we were unhurt but the VW is in a ditch with a damaged axle. Repairs are made the next day in the local town's garage. Not quite impatient but still awaiting Corb's magic, untroubled youth takes a diversion to the cinema to see 'Papa Longues Jambes'. Fred Astaire, was it? Only the French title sticks now.

Next day we make it to Ronchamp at dusk – and yes, it was magical. We stay overnight in the attached hilltop hostel. Next morning over breakfast Paul shows us the grazed arm he suffered from sleeping in a bunk against the rough board-marked concrete walls. Did we think that a letter of complaint to the architect may serve well? Perhaps Monsieur Le Corbusier, from his position on high, smiled gently, knowing that the art of architecture had made itself felt.

1956 Buttons on your Shirt

Left
Le Corbusier's Notre Dame du Haut at Ronchamp (1954).

Leaving our friends in Isfahan at the end of our journey together, Liz and I peeled off to the Iranian oil port of Khorramshah to find a boat to take us south along the east coast of Africa to Capetown.

Trudging daily along the dockside I found nothing but expensive 'offers' from oil tankers, which didn't quite match up to the idea of wending our way in a series of loosely-connected short hops by Arab dhow. With neither the language to communicate nor a dhow in sight we found a kindly consul who listened patiently to the research-based story of our trip so far and our dream of a dhow-shunting voyage. Cautioning us more seriously than I had anticipated, he said that if the dhow adventure was indeed realised (and that itself was doubtful), I would be murdered for the 'buttons on your shirt'. Liz, he suggested, might survive as a young white slave somewhere in North Africa.

So that dream faded. We boarded an oil tanker, but our funds took us only two-thirds of the way, to Madagascar (what happened next is another story). But how might we relate this to architecture? Not obviously or directly. But then there are those common design-related moments, when you're not quite succeeding with one line of thought, one set of ideas, you just go with the flow to move on. I find this an essential part of the process; its not associated with anything like a sense of failure for invariably something relatedly different emerges. And so it goes forward…

Samuel Beckett expressed this feeling succinctly with the reflection: 'Ever tried. Ever failed. No matter. Try again. Fail better'.

In the flow of design, iteration works, stoking the imaginative growth of ideas even when, in Beckett's terms, the result may later come to seem like some kind of 'better fail'.

So whereas Liz and I had to abandon her earlier idea to drive through the heart of Africa, it seemed natural to me to again pick up on the breadth of her intention by suggesting the crazily romantic alternative of hitching on dhows along thousands of miles of the continent's east coast. A late-1960s thought? Yes, but this was in the mid-1950s; another time.

1966 The National Theatre shortlist

As a young practice with few built schemes to our name we were delighted and excited to be invited to attend a shortlist interview for the new National Theatre on London's South Bank.

I visited Berlin to see the opera house, a number of theatres and not least the new Philharmonie by Hans Scharoun, who I was fortunate to meet inside the building. Returning to London, and inspired by the brilliance of Scharoun's auditorium, I made a few sketches of an idea for the National Theatre that had been buzzing around in my mind. A day or two went by, and following a brief discussion with my partners I put a sketch in my jacket pocket as we left for the interview. With no beautiful drawings, no presentation boards, no elegant brochure and certainly no PowerPoint presentation, it seems now like another world. We were three young architects with no experience in this field and not even particularly well versed in theatre – just a small black-ink sketch and some ideas.

Of the interview I remember a large table, no doubt awaiting successive spreads of interesting drawings. We were sat on one side and a welcoming assembly of the great and the good of the UK's theatre world faced us on the other. A lively conversation ranged across the table; the NT's panel with their aspirations for the new theatre, and the three of us with a passion for our work.

When Laurence Olivier asked whether we had any specific proposals, I took the opportunity to lay my very small sketch in the middle of the very large table. The effect was immediate. It was a radical idea for a highly flexible form of auditorium, and a few words and some scratchy black lines on a scrap of paper drew these creative heads together in a surge of interest. Questions and answers flowed. Has it been done before, how would it work? For us it was just an idea in embryo – there were no definitive answers yet, and we must have known that it might not easily work. Yet with youthful confidence we believed something would come of it.

We didn't get the job and, I guess, we hadn't really thought that we would. Rightly, Denys Lasdun did. But it had been a great moment.

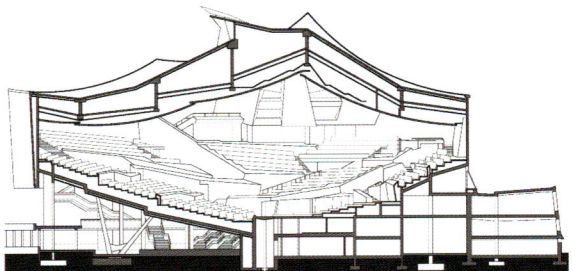

Above
Hans Scharoun's Berlin Philharmonie, sited adjacent to Tiergarten, opened in October 1963. Highly regarded for its acoustics, the main hall placed the orchestra at the heart of the space, surrounded by asymmetrically arranged 'vineyard-style' seating terraces.

Left
Denys Lasdun's National Theatre opened on London's South Bank in 1976.

1968 The Serpentine Cafe competition

In the late-1960s we took part in a limited competition, organised by the government's Property Services Agency, for a new cafe to be situated near the Serpentine bridge in London's Hyde Park. The brief was purposely loose in its requirements and competitors were encouraged to come forward with ideas freely.

This we did, proposing two cafe buildings. The first, near the bridge as requested, was radically structured in glass and raised above the treeline to give views across the park to the skyline beyond. The second, in contrast, was low-lying and at the far end of the Serpentine. An adjacent part of the lake, we suggested, could be frozen in winter to form a skating rink, adding a new dimension to the park.

We were pleased with our two-part proposal and disappointed not to be selected. Apparently our designs were deemed inappropriately ambitious and, in the panel's view, out of keeping with the character of the park. All the more surprising, perhaps, when it was said that ABK had been invited because of our track-record for respecting context.

Why this story? Because whether you're designing a cafe, a college or a crematorium, you do what feels right, all round. Not just to satisfy functionality, what the building is for, but what it's about in the life of the place, the city. This may be perceived as a breaking of an acceptable mould or disturbing expectations. And it may do so; to leave you thinking – perhaps without work.

1976 Beyond a Box

The Dublin-born American architect Kevin Roche, who had completed many interesting projects for Cummins Engines in Columbus, Indiana, recommended ABK to provide advice on an awkward architectural problem at its manufacturing plant at Shotts in the Scottish lowlands. Meeting the Cummins management group at their late-1940s factory building, they explained that the steel-framed extension they planned to build in front of the entrance had not been met with approval by their architecturally-discerning company president.

Shown the design drawings, I was asked whether we could make suggestions to improve the look of the building. Pausing, I asked whether they would first show me around the plant. A moment's surprise was followed by an enthusiastic 'yes', not least because they saw an opportunity to show off the beautiful diesel engines they manufactured there.

Over coffee, I said we wouldn't be able to help 'improve' the proposed building that was on order since, in my view, it really shouldn't be built there at all. Recognising the urgency of their need for expansion, I suggested that they might instead consider asking us to prepare a development plan which could look at all the options for expansion on the site. As our meeting drew to a close I sensed that the idea had sparked some interest.

Cummins became one of our most enlightened corporate clients. They took up our initial proposal for a fundamental analysis of production patterns, and this was followed by the design of a new plan. We went forward together in an extended and fertile dialogue, aiming to satisfy the company's needs in the widest sense.

1986 Dinner with Prince Charles

After the press rumpus surrounding Prince Charles' Hampton Court 'carbuncle' speech, my partners and I thought about how we might make something more positive from it all. Swallowing our pride, we invited the prince to lunch in our office so we might talk about our work. A long silence followed, but eventually I was invited to dinner at Kensington Palace in the company of several other architects. Not quite what we had planned, but why not?

We sat at a round table with about ten guests – I was placed to the left of the prince and Theo Crosby was on his right. Was this significant, I wondered? I knew Theo, not only as an architect and founding partner of Pentagram but later as professor at the Royal College of Art. We three chatted more or less comfortably as the meal progressed until, within a slight silence that hung in our bit of air over the dessert, I quietly asked Theo about the strains of Post-Modernism that, I suggested, had crept into the student work I'd recently seen at the RCA. This raised the temperature a notch or two and we soon found ourselves in a full-blown argument – for me, the Modern Movement was at stake. The Defender of Tradition sat upright between us, perhaps not altogether enjoying this ping-pong argument.

In good time, Theo and I became aware of the need to return to a well-behaved English decorum, regaining our non-combatant cool over coffee, and all may once again have seemed well.

1988 The ANC visits RIBA Council

This was an extra-curriculum activity. Yes, but all such forays fed into the life of our practice, helping to form the diverse and on-the-move character of the place. Small wonder that we were perceived as an off-centre, sometimes unpredictable grouping?

From the mid- to late-1980s I chaired the UK Architects Against Apartheid group (UKAAA), part of the widespread Anti-Apartheid Movement (AAM). In collaboration with the African National Congress we gathered an often supportive response from the architectural profession and, seeking the support of the RIBA Council in relation to, for instance, the cultural and academic boycott, we found a sympathetic ear in the then RIBA president Max Hutchinson.

We were invited to make a presentation to members of the council in their chamber and, I informed them, we would be accompanied by Mendi Msimeng, the ANC's chief representative in exile in the UK. What could not have been foreseen was that, as a result of a recent arson attack on the ANC's head office, extra security arrangements had been put in place. Much as we would have wished it otherwise, the ANC's bodyguards formed a substantial part of our party's presence in this inner sanctum. For a while, the RIBA councillors' bums seemed to move a little restlessly on their seats but, as we made our informal presentation, it must have become apparent that we weren't terrorists and that the room was not about to become a war zone. On leaving the building we felt grateful to the president and this progressive group of architects that our ideas and proposals had been well received.

Just six years later, after South Africa's first multi-racial elections, the ANC formed a new government. Metamorphosis.

2003 The Big Arts Week

This piece touches on the delight and privilege of working for short spells with school children. In 2003 I took part in a week-long summer activity organised by the Big Arts Week for 10-year-olds at Primrose Hill Primary School in north London. In collaboration with their class teacher, I suggested a project type that lay beyond the boundaries of the school's normal curriculum. A day-by-day film of the event was made by Richard Cooper.

The idea was to involve the whole class, as well as each child individually, in a project related to architectural design, but using neither that description nor any related professional jargon.

With Mark Fineberg, I'd collected (or recycled) a load of used cardboard fruit and vegetable boxes from the local market. Beside the playground, in the Victorian school's colonnaded undercroft, we set out two crescent-like alignments of open boxes, each awaiting inhabitation so as to form a 'common' between the two 'terraces'.

After we had taped the boxes together to make a sufficiently stable structure, the children were invited to choose the space in which they would each make their 'place for precious things' – things that had personal meanings for them and which they'd make or represent in different forms in the days ahead.

Whereas the girls seemed to choose a wide variety of subjects, many of the boys focussed on differing representations of football. Towards the close of our set of workshops we invited each pupil to talk about their installation as we stood listening in the common space, a celebration of individual effort in relation to the work as a whole. In the final few hours, one boy, who had earlier made it clear that he was not keen to get involved with the project at all, suddenly set to with a brush, painting the outer

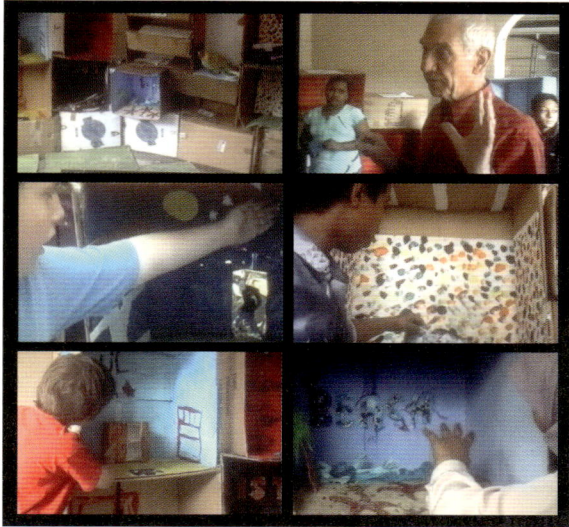

faces of the boxed structures in a variety of colours. With both determination and energy, his decidedly alternative contribution was applied to the whole rather than the part – a striking reminder of the value of both presenting other viewpoints and doing things differently.

Somewhere out there, I imagine him now, more than a decade later, a young man, a strategist, or perhaps an architecture student?

Togetherness, Differences, Unpredictability

By way of an interlude I thought to say something about Richard, Paul and myself in the context of our work and, by implication, about our group practice, a longstanding and active threesome which, in the structure of this book, can be seen as a significant parallel reading of its title, A3.

In analysing the work of poet Robert Frost, Clive James suggested that 'in whatever form he chose, writing a poem, not just writing poetry, was what Frost was after'. Likewise for ABK, it was the focus and character of a particular design that mattered rather more than any contribution we might make to architectural culture at large. In 'Collaborations' (2002), Paul Finch describes how 'each ABK building is a separate story', characterising our individual contributions by imagining one of us 'getting ready to sound the drum', while another 'ponders on the nature of the drum' and the third 'wonders whether actually a trumpet may be more appropriate'. He concludes that 'if one were to look for a single word to summarise the nature of their collaborations and, most important, the built outcomes, I would choose "unpredictable", in its most constructive and positive sense'.

This touches on some of the fundamental aspects of what our work has been about. For it was little concerned with process-formulations or carefully-drafted policies but rather the exploration and discovery (both by digging and osmosis, perhaps) of the latent opportunities within each project-related 'context'. This would range from people and their sometimes elusive aspirations to the material stuff of putting things together to make buildings.

The design process is nothing if not dynamic, for on occasions unexpected changes can occur in a brief, either as a result of the design dialogue or for reasons lying outside that process. A scheme's focus may need to shift, for instance with a doubling (or halving) of the accomodation requirements, a newly expressed need for construction phasing, or by further analysis a client may arrive at an alternative or more appropiate set of needs. After a pause we would often hear: 'can you start tomorrow', or 'how can this be phased?' The conceptual design ideas still floating around in your head start to move, as if by their own energy, in a loose-coupled dance with the new external forces that are already stepping out to their own rhythm.

Such are some of the threads that bound us in our web of understanding, working within an open framework of intense togetherness, nurturing and testing ideas. Sometimes they'd take hold and materialise but at other times they wouldn't. That too may be described as inherently unpredictable in the making of architecture.

Presence and Absence

Having followed this passage across almost a century, we reach the present time and the near closure of this journey with a sense of ambiguity, considering representations of 'presence' and 'absence' as a kind of togetherness. It seems an appropriate point to introduce some ideas I've been working on for abstract sculptural installations that explore the complex relationship of 'presence' and 'absence' through dualities: seen/unseen, life/death, physicality/abstraction, democracy/fascism, night/day, summer/winter. My interest lies not in one or other of these opposing states but rather in the observation that we live with realities that contain contradiction. So I thought to make an installation that takes presence and absence as an underlying theme, and gives form, materiality and expression to this common condition.

These ideas are no more than work in progress, and I wouldn't want to exaggerate their significance. But a spacious place to show the work would be good! Not too smart, so everyone can enter at ease, and without the intimidations of 'high culture' often associated with galleries in which hardly a word can be spoken above a whisper – ordinariness would be a strong asset. In illustrating these models I feel that I needn't say more – things should speak for themselves, and either reach you or not.

I've made a set of planes, like thin slices of our lives perhaps, or walls, a common architectural element of material substance. Holes are cut in them, like absent heads or maybe continents surrounded by oceans. The cut-out bits remain, semi-detached in displaced positions with mirrored outer surfaces reflecting our image as we pass by; the attendant masks present an alternative presence.

It's as though they've not come to stay. Absent friends perhaps, offering another set of presences; unexpected alternatives, or an absence suggesting the significance of memory?

Mike Jay's essay, Argument with Myself, is pertinent in this respect: 'Memory creates our identity, but it also exposes the illusion of a coherent self: a memory is not a thing but an act that alters and rearranges even as it retrieves. Although some of its operations can be trained to an astonishing pitch, most take place autonomously, beyond the reach of the conscious mind. As we age, it distorts and foreshortens: present experience becomes harder to impress on the mind, and the long-forgotten past seems to draw closer.' (London Review of Books, 23 May 2013).

Two further ideas before closing. Years ago I worked on the idea of presenting urban artworks in which images in the form of after-dusk illuminations are projected onto large bodies of water. These would be temporary but grand in scale and open to all passing by. If in London they could be located along the stretches between the Thames bridges, on the Serpentine lake or the Royal Docks in Newham – ThamesAlight, perhaps, LiffeyAlight in Dublin or SpreeAlight in Berlin. The London mayor's office wasn't then that interested, but with key figures in the Dublin City Council we came close to implementing a trial-run for the Liffey. But then, as often seems the case, the funding was withdrawn.

Sad, but things change and sometimes you find that others take up the ideas, perhaps dressed in a different costume, when the time is right. When ABK worked on London's Docklands Light Railway stations 25 years ago, I suggested that, in addition to our kit-of-parts design language, each station should be celebrated and made unique by a work of public

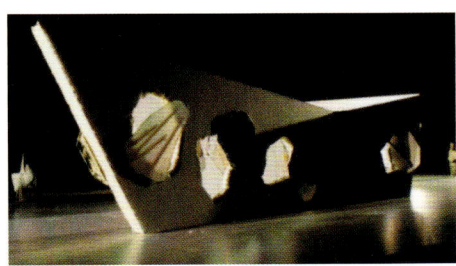

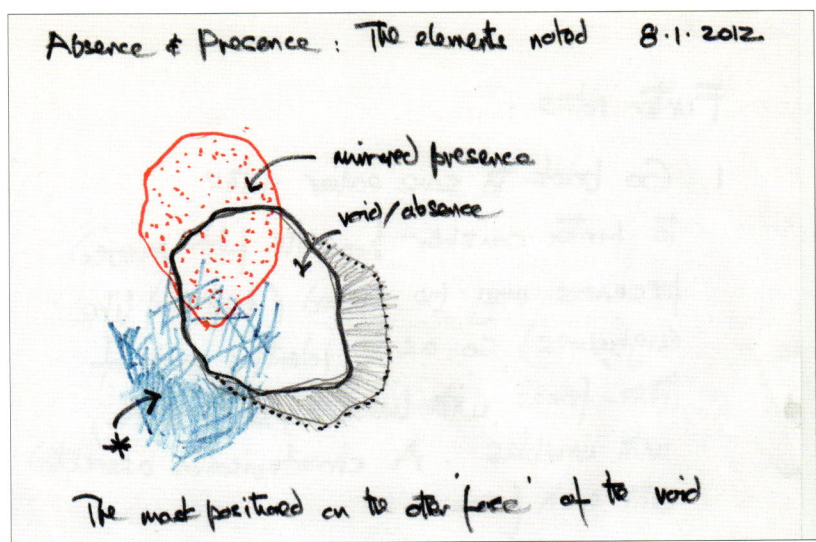

Above/right
Working models exhibiting the ideas of absence and presence in relation to their freestanding walls that, in themselves, stand as planes of presence.

Right
An exploratory sketch considering the juxtaposition and arrangement of elements, noting their materialities.

Left
LiffeyAlight envisages illuminations projected onto Dublin's river.

art relating to the character of the locality. Funding was refused, but I understand there's been a recent move to adopt the idea – better to have ideas that materialise late than not at all.

I'm now working on another set of ideas, but not for city-scale art. Modest-sized collaged sheets of translucent paper, drawings reflecting abstractions of possible superimpositions; past and present urban layers upon the surface of our globe; presence and absence figured as essential elements of our heritage. These are early days for this work in progress; another small journey unravelling a personal need to see and say, bumping along within the medium to find a sense of space in which the mind may roam.

As a young man, fifty years ago, I was occasionally 'presented' with a recurring dream of a type, I appreciate, that may be well known to psychoanalysts and sci-fi enthusiasts. I found myself moving through the limitless expanse of the outer space of our universe (dark-energied multi-verses?), effortlessly and alone, skying with neither wings nor the propelling use of my limbs – Superman, no less! By the decision-making power of my mind alone I could, with an almost detached and modest sense of curiosity, go anywhere, roaming free without a 'plan' in time and through space, no boundaries.

Now, I imagine myself looking back to Earth over my dream-shoulder, just able to see small grains of sand on the surface of our planet. And by the magic of an internalised and new-found X-raying magnification, I'm delighted to recognise these distant specks as some of ABK's buildings. Looking again at our work from this distance I'm taken back to our searching design consultations and discussions, hoping that in those efforts to fulfil shared aspirations with many others we made good architecture, bringing meaningful new places into the stuff of people's lives.

Returning to my dream-journey I feel as though I am both 'here' and, by means of this seemingly undirected dream-flight, also out 'there'; like sub-atomic particles (neutrinos and others) to whom this brief description of interplanetary travel may seem to be no more than their routine experience of cross-spatial behaviour.

Architects, are they?

Visiting other galaxies. Any time.

Bruno Ahrends (9th April 1878–24th July 1948), the son of Berlin banker Barthold and Bertha Arons, was brought up in Villa Arons in the Colonie Alsen on the Wannsee. His uncle was the financier and arts patron James Simon.

Having been barred from studying shipbuilding at Kiel, Ahrends studied architecture at the Technischen Universität München and the Technische Hochschule Charlottenburg. After graduating in 1903 he worked as an apprentice in the public works department, graduating to Regierungsbaumeister. In 1904 he changed his name to Ahrends (after he and his siblings converted to Christianity), and married Johanna Springer, granddaughter of publisher Julius Springer. He worked as an independent architect in Berlin until banned in 1935 because of his Jewish roots. In 1936 he fled to Italy and in 1939 to Britain, where his daughter was living. As a former German soldier, he was interned on the Isle of Man. In 1948 he emigrated to Cape Town, where he died soon afterwards.

Steffen Ahrends was born in Berlin on 16th August 1907. He attended school in Landheim Schondorf, Bavaria before studying architecture at the University of Berlin-Charlottenburg (1924-25) and the Bauhochschule Weimar under Otto Bartning and Ernst Neufert (1925-29). After emigrating to South Africa in 1936, he sat a special examination at the University of Witwatersrand, Johannesburg in 1937, gaining a diploma in architecture in 1938. He married Margarete Marie Sophie Visino in 1930 (divorced 1944), Ruth Napier 1946 (divorced 1963), and Jackie Popper in 1964; his children were Peter, Benjamin, Sebastian and Katrina.

Steffen worked in his father Bruno's studio in Berlin from 1930-36, with an interim period in Ernst May's Group in Moscow (1931-32). He worked in private practice in Johannesburg from 1938, in partnership with Robin Walker (1948-53), Michael Sutton (1952-64), Trevor Wellbeloved (1965-78) and Adrian van Dongen (1969-78), and in Spain with Aubrey David from 1972-75 and from 1978 until his death on 31st October 1992.

1911-12 Ahrends House Miquelstraße, Berlin-Dahlem.
1912-33 House group, Im Gehege, Berlin-Dahlem. (Heinrich Schweitzer and Bruno Ahrends).
1919-27 Houses, Johannisthal Siedlung, Breiter Weg.
1920 House, Adelheidallee, Berlin-Tegel.
1920-21 Houses, Zabel-Krüger-Damm, Berlin-Lübars.
1921-25 Ahrends house, Am Großen Wannsee, Berlin.
1922 House, Herrnholzweg, Berlin-Lübars.
1924-25 House, Zehntwerderweg, Berlin-Lübars.
1924-28, Houses, Forststraße, Berlin-Steglitz.
1925-27, Frieda-Köpcke-Haus and rental apartments, Scharfestraße, Berlin-Zehlendorf.
1925-30 Rupprechtblöcke, Berlin-Lichtenberg.
1925-30 Houses, Archibaldweg, Berlin-Rummelsburg.
1926-27 Meeting house, Schuchardtweg, Berlin-Wannsee.
1927-28 Haus Krüger, Wachtelstraße, Berlin-Dahlem.
1927-28 House Kyllmannstraße, Berlin-Wannsee.
1927-29 Apartment building, Cunostraße, Berlin-Schmargendorf.
1929 Primus apartment building, Christianenstraße, Berlin-Merseburg.
1929-31 Weiße Stadt Siedlung, Aroser Allee, Berlin-Reinickendorf (Ahrends, Bruno & Büning, Wilhelm & Salvisberg, Otto Rudolf).
1930 Shop and garage, Wiener Straße, Berlin-Kreuzberg
1934 House, Edelhofdamm, Berlin-Frohnau.

1938-78 500 houses in Transvaal, Cape Province, Natal Province, Orange Free State and Rhodesia.
1950 Clubhouse, Bryanston Country Club, Sandton, Transvaal; Huntingdon Shops and flats, Sandown, Transvaal.
1951 Matus shops and offices, Roodepoort, Transvaal; Revolf shops and flats, Greenside, Johannesburg.
1952 Gols and Diamond Pavilions, Van Riebeck Festival, Cape Town.
1952-60 Suzmann Showroom, warehouse and offices, Welkom, Orange Free State and Pretoria, Ermel and Bethal, Transvaal.
1953 Transvaal Chamber of Mines Pavilion, Rand Show, Johannesburg; Bryanston Country Club reconstruction, Sandton, Transvaal.
1954 Engelhard Court House, Hurlingham, Transvaal; Bedelia Hotel, Welkom, Orange Free State; Daagbreek Hotel, Welkom, Orange Free State; Transvaal Chamber of Mines Pavilion, Bloemfontein, Orange Free State and Bulawayo, Rhodesia; BSA Pavilion, Bulawayo, Rhodesia.
1955 Harmony Hotel, Virginia, Orange Free State; Housing, Benoni, Transvaal.
1958 Engelhard Guest House, Sabie River Bungalow, Transvaal; Anglo-American Corporation Guest House, Welkom, Orange Free State; Fibro Service Station, Bedfordview, Transvaal; Balalaika Hotel, Sandown, Johannesburg.
1959 Total Oil Service Station, Fairview, Johannesburg; Callinicos shops and flats, Kensington, Johannesburg.
1960 Barlows (Caterpillar) BT & M Factory, Isando, Transvaal.
1961 Total Oil Service Station, Illovo, Johannesburg; Bayers Agrochem factory, Isando, Transvaal.

1962 Barclays Bank, Louis Trichard, Transvaal; Sanipass Hotel, Drakensberg, Natal.
1962-72 T&C office and warehouse, Isando, Transvaal.
1962-78 Clubhouse, Johannesburg Turf Club.
1963 Drum Rock Hotel, White River, Transvaal; Commissioner General's residences, Mafeking, Cape Province; Social Science & Speech Clinic, University of Witwatersrand, Johannesburg; Transvaal Provincial Administration hostels and schools in Witbank, Sanieshof, Klersdorf, Koster and Coligny, Transvaal.
1963-69 CPL (Agfa) factory, Isando, Transvaal.
1964 Barclays Bank Pavilion, Rand Show, Johannesburg; Sturrock & Robson Guest House, Dullstrom, Transvaal; Sabie Country Club House, Sabie, Transvaal; Barlows (Caterpilar) BT&M Factory, Belleville, Cape Province.
1965 Barlows (Hyster) Factory, Isando, Transvaal; Barlows Federated Timber Factory, Benoni, Transvaal; Gallo Pavilion, Rand Show, Johannesburg.
1966 Mbula Guest House, Sabie, Transvaal.
1967 River Club House, Sandton, Transvaal; Barlows Federated Timber Factory, Springs, Transvaal.
1968 T&C Office and warehouse, Paarl, Cape Province.
1970 SAFI offices, Sabie, Transvaal.
1971 T&C offices and warehouse, Milnerton, Cape Province; CPL (Agfa) factory, Milnerton, Cape Province; three houses at Sotogrande, Costa del Sol, Spain.
1972-75 Bahia de Casares housing, Estepona, Costa del Sol, Spain (with Aubrey David).
1974 Guest house, Piggs Peak, Swaziland.

Peter Ahrends was born in Berlin on 30th April 1933 to Steffen and Visino Ahrends. From the age of four he was brought up in Johannesburg and, after his parents divorced when he was 11, attended boarding school. He moved to London in 1951 to study at the Architectural Association, qualifying in 1959. With fellow students Richard Burton and Paul Koralek he won first prize in the competition for the Berkeley Library at Trinity College, Dublin, setting up Ahrends Burton Koralek (ABK) in 1961. He married Elizabeth Robertson in 1954, and has two daughters.

Peter was a member of the Architectural Association council (1965-67), the Design Council (1988-93), and chairman of UK Architects Against Apartheid (1986-94). His academic posts include visiting professor at Kingston Polytechnic (1984-85), and professor at the Bartlett School of Architecture & Planning at University College London (1986-89). He has held other part-time teaching posts, been an external examiner and held workshops in the UK, Africa, Hong Kong and Canada.

ABK – selected works

1961 Bryan Brown House, Devon.
1961-67 Berkeley Library, Trinity College, Dublin.
1961-65 Study and residences, Chichester Theological College.
1963 Kasmin Gallery, London.
1964 St Anne's Church, Soho, London.
1965-72 Roman Catholic Chaplaincy, Oxford.
1966-69 Dunstan Road houses, Oxford.
1966-71 Redcar Library, North Yorkshire.
1966-73 Maidenhead Library, Berkshire.
1968 Thurmaston School, Leicestershire.
1968 Canberra Bell Tower competition.
1968-72 St Andrew's College, Booterstown, Dublin.
1968-72 Nebenzahl House, Jerusalem.
1968-77 Chalvedon Housing, Basildon, Essex.
1968-79 Arts Faculty building, Trinity College, Dublin.
1969-96 Templeton College, Oxford.
1972-80 Residences, Keble College, Oxford.
1972-74 Habitat store and warehouse, Wallingford.
1973-90 Portsmouth Polytechnic Library, Hampshire.
1975-83 Cummins Engines Factory, Shotts, Lanarkshire.
1975 Post Office Headquarters, London.
1977 British Airports Authority head office, Gatwick, West Sussex.
1979-90 John Lewis department store, Kingston-upon-Thames, Surrey.
1980 Mary Rose Museum, Portsmouth, Hampshire.
1982-84 Sainsbury supermarket, Canterbury, Kent.
1982-85 National Gallery extension, London.
1982-85 WH Smith headquarters, Swindon, Wiltshire.
1982-90 St Mary's Hospital, Isle of Wight.
1983-90 Hooke Park College, Dorset.
1983 British Telecom headquarters, Milton Keynes.
1986-2002 Burton House, London.
1986 Shaftesbury Avenue offices, London.
1987-93 Beckton Extension and Poplar Bridge, Docklands Light Railway, London.
1988-90 Dover Heritage Centre, Kent.
1988-2000 British Embassy, Moscow, Russia.
1990 Grenoble University masterplan, France.
1991-98 Dublin Dental Hospital.
1991-99 Whitworth Art Gallery development plan and sculpture court, Manchester.
1992-95 Techniquest Science Discovery Centre, Cardiff.
1994-96 WH Smith headquarters extension, Swindon, Wiltshire.
1995-97 Selly Oak Colleges LRC, Birmingham.
1996-2001 Institute of Technology, Tralee, County Kerry.
1997-98 Waterford Visitor Centre, Ireland.
1998-2002 Blanchardstown Institute of Technology, Dublin.
1999-2002 Offaly Council Offices, Ireland.
2003 Bexhill mixed-use project, Sussex.
2004 Lower Lea Valley study, London.
2004-07 Cork Civic Offices, Ireland.

Image credits

ABK Archive and Peter Ahrends: 11(r), 17, 19, 30, 32-33, 38, 39 (tl), 40 (t, br), 42, 47 (l), 53, 75-85, 88-111, 123, 124.

John Donat (ABK/RIBA Library Photographs Collection/Architectural Association): 35, 36, 37 (b), 43, 44, 45, 46 (t, m), 48 (m), 50, 51 (t), 54 (t), 55, 58, 59 (tl, ml), 67 (tr, mr), 69, 70 (t, m), 71 (tr, br), 73.

John Donat: 39 (tr, br, bl), 40 (bl), 41, 56 (m).

Architectural Association (ABK Collection): 11(l), 34 (Valerie Bennett/National Portrait Gallery), 47 (tr, bl), 48 (t Charlotte Wood), 48 (b), 49 (Peter Cook), 52 (b Terry Grimwood), 59 (mr), 60 (Christian Richters), 62, 64, 65, 67 (bl Martin Charles), 68 (b), 70 (m), 72 (Peter Cook).

Antoine Raffoul (ABK/Architectural Association): 37 (t), 46 (br), 47 (m, br), 52 (t, m), 63, 66, 67 (tl, ml), 68 (t), 71 (tl, ml).

Anti-apartheid Movement Archives: 14; Richard Burton: 28, 51 (b), 70 (b Richard O Davies), 109 (b); Christine Cadin: 112; Richard Cooper: 119; Habitat: 61; Hans Freytag: 114; George Kasabov: 10; Walter Knirr/City of Johannesburg: 20; Ian Latham: 23; LDA (Landesamtes für Denkmalpflege und Archäologie Sachsen-Anhalt) Archiv/Bittner: 86, 87; Manor Studio: 24-26; Sue Ream (Creative Commons): 8; Simonopetra Monastery/Thodoris Lakiotis (Creative Commons): 113; South Bank Centre: 116.

Quotations on Bruno Ahrends (pp79-82) by Klaus Hinrichsen (1912-2004) are the copyright of his estate.

Unless otherwise stated, images are from Peter Ahrends/ABK Archive. Copyright holders have been traced wherever possible; we apologise for any inadvertent misattribution.

Copyright ©2015 Right Angle Publishing
Edited and designed by Ian Latham

All rights reserved. No part of this publication may be reproduced in any manner whatsoever without prior permission in writing from Right Angle Publishing.

First published by Right Angle Publishing (London)

British Library Cataloguing in Publication Data
A catalogue record for this book is available from the British Library

ISBN-13: 978-0-9532848-9-4